Fondue

D0376366

Recipe	Page	Calories per serving	easy	kids love it	takes a while	sophisticated	low-cal	vegetarian	can prepare in advance	inexpensive
Cheese Fondue with Leeks and Ham	6	1200	●			●				
Three-Cheese Fondue	6	1070	●					●		
Cheese Fondue with Porcini Mushrooms	8	1045	●			●		●		
Tomato-Cheese Fondue	8	1065	●					●	●	●
Sheep's Cheese Fondue	10	780	●					●	●	
Cheese Curry Fondue	12	760	●	●		●		●		
Cheese and Herb Fondue	12	760	●			●		●		
Normandy Fondue	12	1180	●			●		●		
Cheese-Walnut Fondue	14	750	●					●		●
Mushroom-Cheese Fondue	14	1040	●			●		●		
Meatball Fondue	18	1050	●			●			●	
Tex-Mex Fondue	20	1040			●	●			●	
Traditional Meat Fondue	20	1020	●	●		●			●	
Poultry Fondue with Artichokes	21	850	●						●	●
Rustic Meat Fondue	22	1510	●	●					●	●
Potato Fondue	22	995	●	●					●	●
Duck Fondue	24	805			●	●			●	
Crunchy Vegetable Fondue	25	830	●					●	●	●
Chips & Dips	26	850	●						●	
Fish Fondue	30	370			●	●			●	
Curried Seafood Fondue	30	1020	●			●	●		●	
Chile-Spiked Pork Fondue	32	490			●	●			●	
Dumpling Fondue	33	470	●			●	●		●	
Family-Style Fondue	34	945		●	●				●	

Recipe

Recipe	Page	Calories per serving	easy	kids love it	takes a while	sophisticated	low-cal	vegetarian	can prepare in advance	inexpensive
Smoked Pork Fondue	34	1055	●	●					●	
Venison Fondue	36	450	●			●	●		●	
Wine Fondue	36	890	●			●			●	
Vegetable Fondue with Three Sauces	38	785	●	●					●	●
Viennese Fondue	38	970			●	●			●	
Chinese Hot Pot	42	440			●	●	●			
Korean Hot Pot	44	470	●			●	●			
Mongolian Hot Pot	44	820	●			●		●		
Shabu Shabu	46	450				●	●		●	
Sukiyaki	46	640	●			●			●	
Bagna Cauda	48	1240	●						●	●
American-Style Fondue	49	850	●	●					●	
Swiss Cheese Fondue	50	1185	●					●		●
Fonduta	50	940	●			●		●		●
Sweet & Spicy Vegetables	54	190	●			●	●	●	●	●
Zucchini Relish	54	230	●			●		●	●	●
Tomato-Cucumber Chutney	56	70	●				●	●	●	●
Onion Chutney	56	85	●			●	●	●	●	●
Apple-Ginger Chutney	57	240	●			●		●	●	●
Pineapple Chutney	57	190	●			●	●	●	●	
Potato-Garlic Sauce	58	145	●				●			●
Parsley-Walnut Pesto	58	375				●		●	●	
Chocolate Fondue	60	650	●	●		●				
Exotic Coconut Fondue	61	275	●	●		●	●			

When served authentically, cheese fondue is placed on the table in a ceramic or earthenware pot, called a *caquelon* in Switzerland. The glazed, heatproof material that composes the pot slowly absorbs the heat and gently transfers it to the cheese. A pot with a polished bottom that you can set it directly on the stove is best. Make sure the bottom of the pot has the same diameter as the burner on your stove. Otherwise the pot may crack. If necessary, you can also prepare cheese fondue in a regular saucepan or meat fondue pot. Take care not to let it get too hot or the cheese will stick.

Most Important: Good Cheese

Cheese fondue is only as good as the cheese you put in it—so always choose the best. For better melting, choose unsliced cheese and cut it into cubes or shred it. Semi-hard and hard cheese with a fat content of 45% or more is especially good for melting. Good choices include Emmenthaler, Gruyère, Appenzeller, cheddar, and Gouda. The younger the cheese, the milder the flavor of the fondue will be. The older the cheese, the richer the flavor and creamier the texture the fondue will be. You can mix up to 3 varieties of cheeses, which have been aged for different lengths of time for a fondue.

Cheese Fondues

Three varieties of cheese that are good for melting: left rear, Appenzeller; middle, cheddar; right, Emmenthaler

Wine

To prepare a traditional cheese fondue, you should use a high-quality, dry white wine. This is one of the major elements contributing to the success of your fondue. The wine's natural acidity makes the cheese smooth and creamy and keeps it from becoming runny. Therefore, young wine is best; very old wine generally isn't acidic enough. To be on the safe side, you can add 1 or 2 teaspoons of lemon juice to your fondue. Hard cider—fermented apple juice—makes an excellent cheese fondue. Or, you can use regular apple cider, which is an excellent alternative when eating fondue with children. If you're using another liquid such as beer, always add 1 tbs of lemon juice.

Bread

Good bread choices for fondue are virtually limitless. Any type can be used, from fluffy, white bread to heavy, whole-grain bread. A creative way to present cheese fondue is with a variety of fresh, crusty white bread and multi-grain bread with nuts and spices. When you cut the bread, try to make sure it still has a portion of the crust. This will give it stability on the fondue fork, keeping the bread from falling off.

The Right Stirring Technique

In order to keep the cheese from forming clumps while it's melting, always stir it with a spoon in a figure-eight pattern.

Fondue has the best consistency when the cheese mixture is smooth and creamy, and softly coats the bread without dripping too much. The fondue should always be bubbling gently on the heat source, but should never get too hot. To keep the fondue creamy right down to the last bite, stir the fondue throughout the meal. Even when you're eating, stir the bread or vegetables around vigorously in the cheese in a figure-eight pattern and rotate your wrist slightly as you lift it out.

Tips and Tricks
• Count on supplying 5-7 oz each of cheese and bread per person.
• The amount of liquid required for a cheese fondue recipe will be equal to half the amount of cheese.
• If the consistency of the fondue is too thin, stir in more grated cheese. If it's too thick, thin it with a little warm white wine.

• If the cheese fondue should become runny, add a little cornstarch mixed with wine or water and bring it to a boil briefly while stirring the fondue constantly.

What to Drink

The ideal companion to cheese fondue is the wine that was used to prepare it. For a nonalcoholic choice, try high-quality black tea. Afterwards, a little brandy or kirsch is nice, because such drinks aid the digestion process.

Light or dark, airy or dense—a variety of breads works well in cheese fondue

Cheese Fondue with Leeks and Ham

- easy
- ● sophisticated

Serves 4:
18 oz dark multigrain bread
14 oz cooked ham (fat trimmed)
16 oz cheddar cheese (orange colored)
7 oz Tilsit or Gouda cheese
1 small leek
1 tbs butter
2 tsp flour
10 oz light beer (regular or non-alcoholic)
1-2 tbs fresh lemon juice
Pepper to taste
Freshly ground nutmeg to taste

Prep time: 50 minutes
Per serving approx.: 1200 calories / 68 g protein / 69 g fat / 69 g carbohydrates

1 Preheat the oven to 350°F. Cut the bread into approximately 3/4-inch cubes and place in a single layer on an ungreased baking sheet. Toast the bread, in batches if necessary, until golden brown on all sides. Cut the ham into cubes slightly smaller than the bread. Arrange the bread and ham on separate serving dishes.

2 Remove the rinds from the cheeses, and coarsely grate them or dice them finely. Trim the leek, quarter it lengthwise, wash it well (remember to get between the layers) and cut it into thin slices. In a saucepan, heat the butter over low heat. Add the leek, cover the pan, and simmer the mixture for 3 minutes.

3 Dust the leek with flour and sauté briefly, until slightly browned. Add the beer and lemon juice, cover, and bring to a boil over medium heat.

4 Gradually add the cheeses and cook over low heat, stirring constantly in a figure-eight pattern. Continue stirring until you have a thick, creamy mixture. Season the cheese mixture generously with pepper and a dash of nutmeg, and transfer the mixture to a preheated fondue pot. Place the fondue pot on the table over the heat source.

> **Tip!** For a zestier fondue, stir a little spicy mustard into the cheese mixture.

Three-Cheese Fondue

- easy
- ● vegetarian

Serves 4:
24 oz dense multi-grain bread
8 oz raclette cheese
8 oz garlic-pepper Monterey Jack cheese
5 oz goat cheese
1 clove garlic
1 1/4 cups dry white wine
2 tsp cornstarch
2 tsp lemon juice
1/4 cup apple brandy or fruit brandy
White pepper to taste
Freshly grated nutmeg to taste
2 tbs chopped fresh Italian parsley

Prep time: 30 minutes
Per serving approx.: 1070 calories / 51 g protein / 44 g fat / 96 g carbohydrates

1 Cut the bread into finger-width slices, then into bite-sized chunks. Arrange the bread in a basket or serving dish.

2 Remove the rinds from the cheeses and dice them. Peel the garlic.

3 Pour 1/4 cup of the wine into a small bowl or cup, add the cornstarch, and stir until smooth.

4 Pour the remaining 1 cup wine and the lemon juice into cheese fondue pot and bring to a boil. Mince the garlic and add it to the pot. Gradually add the diced cheese to the pot and cook over medium heat, stirring constantly in a figure-eight pattern, until the mixture is smooth and creamy.

5 Add the cornstarch mixture and brandy to the fondue and bring to a rolling boil, stirring constantly. Season the mixture with pepper and nutmeg. Stir in the parsley. Place the fondue pot on the table over the heat source.

6 To eat, spear the bread cubes with fondue forks and dip them in the cheese mixture.

Serving suggestion: This tastes good with Sweet & Spicy Vegetables or Zucchini Relish (p 54).

Clockwise from top left: Cheese Fondue with Leek and Ham, Zucchini Relish, Three-Cheese Fondue

Cheese Fondue with Porcini Mushrooms

● easy
● sophisticated

Serves 4:
14 oz porcini mushrooms
  (or other mushrooms)
2 shallots
1 clove garlic
2 tbs canola oil
2 tbs fresh lemon juice
Salt & white pepper to
  taste
1 large baguette
10 oz or Gruyère cheese
10 oz Emmenthaler cheese
2 tsp cornstarch
1 1/4 cups dry white wine
2 tbs small fresh Italian
  parsley leaves

Prep time: 50 minutes
Per serving approx.: 1045
calories / 56 g protein / 52 g fat
/ 74 g carbohydrates

1 If necessary, rinse the mushrooms quickly under cold water and pat dry. Trim the mushrooms and cut them into large slices. Peel the shallots and garlic. Mince the shallots.

2 In a skillet, heat the oil over medium-high heat. Add the mushrooms and shallots and sauté for 5 minutes, until golden brown. Stir in 1 tbs of the lemon juice, and season with salt and pepper. Cut the baguette into bite-sized chunks.

3 Remove the rinds from the cheeses and dice them. Place 1/4 cup of the wine in a small bowl or cup, add the cornstarch, and stir until smooth. Halve the garlic lengthwise and rub it vigorously around the inside of the cheese fondue pot.

4 Pour the remaining 1 cup white wine and 1 tbs lemon juice into the fondue pot and bring to a boil over medium heat. Gradually add the diced cheese, and cook over low heat, stirring constantly in a figure-eight pattern, until the mixture is smooth and creamy.

5 Add the cornstarch mixture and bring the cheese mixture to a boil, stirring constantly. Stir in the mushrooms and parsley, and season to taste with pepper. Place the fondue pot on the table over the heat source.

6 To eat, spear the bread chunks with fondue forks and dip in the cheese-mushroom mixture.

Tomato-Cheese Fondue

● vegetarian
● inexpensive

Serves 4:
2 1/4 lb mixed vegetables
  (such as cauliflower,
  broccoli, green onions,
  and bell peppers)
Salt to taste
1 baguette
3 ripe tomatoes
14 oz Appenzeller cheese
8 oz raclette cheese
1 clove garlic
2 tsp cornstarch
2 tsp fresh lemon juice
1 1/4 cups dry white wine
1/4 cup tomato paste
1 tsp dried thyme
Pepper to taste

Prep time: 1 1/4 hours
Per serving approx.: 1065
calories / 61 g protein / 61 g fat
/ 85 g carbohydrates

1 Trim and wash all of the vegetables, peel if necessary, and cut them into bite-sized pieces. Plunge the vegetables (except bell peppers), one type at a time, into boiling salted water until partially cooked (blanched). For example, cook cauliflower for about 10 minutes, broccoli stalks for about 5 minutes, broccoli florets for about 3 minutes, and green onions for about 1 minute. Remove the vegetables from the boiling water and place them in a bowl of ice water to cool; drain thoroughly. On serving dishes or in bowls, arrange all of the vegetables. Cut the bread into bite-sized chunks and arrange in a basket.

2 Dip the tomatoes into boiling water for 15-30 seconds to loosen the skins, then plunge them into cold water. With a paring knife, pull off the tomato skins, cut the tomatoes in half, squeeze out the seeds, and dice the tomato flesh.

3 Remove the rinds from the cheeses, and grate them coarsely. Peel the garlic and halve lengthwise. Vigorously rub the garlic around the inside of a cheese fondue pot.

4 Place 1/4 cup of the wine in a small bowl or cup, add the cornstarch, and stir until smooth. Pour the remaining 1 cup wine, the lemon juice, tomato paste, and thyme into the fondue pot and bring to a boil over medium heat. Gradually add the cheese and cook over low heat, stirring

constantly in a figure-eight pattern, until the mixture is smooth and creamy.

5 As soon as cheese mixture bubbles, fold in the tomatoes and the cornstarch mixture. Bring all ingredients to a boil, stirring constantly, and season to taste with pepper. Place the fondue pot on the table over the heat source.

6 To eat, spear the bread chunks and vegetables with fondue forks and dip in the cheese-tomato mixture.

Variations

You can use other types of cheese for this fondue, such as Emmenthaler, medium-aged Gouda, or Gruyère. For a different flavor, use pureed roasted red peppers instead of tomato paste.

above: **Cheese Fondue with Porcini Mushrooms**
below: **Tomato–Cheese Fondue**

Sheep's Cheese Fondue

● easy
● vegetarian

Serves 4:
2 small zucchini
1 small eggplant
5 tbs olive oil
1 red bell pepper
2 loaves sesame flatbread
5 oz olives
14 oz hard sheep's cheese
  (such as Manchego)
10 oz soft, mild sheep's
  cheese (such as feta)
1 small onion
1-2 cloves garlic
1 1/4 cups vegetable stock
1 tbs fresh lemon juice
1 tsp dried oregano
1 tbs cornstarch
Pepper to taste
2 tbs chopped fresh Italian
  parsley

Prep time: 50 minutes
Per serving approx.: 780 calories
/ 31 g protein / 54 g fat / 48 g
carbohydrates

1 Wash the zucchini
and eggplant; cut them
into 1/2-inch cubes. In a
large skillet, heat 2 tbs of
the oil over medium heat.
Add the zucchini and
sauté until golden.
Transfer the zucchini to
paper towels to drain.
Sauté the eggplant with 2
tbs more olive oil.

2 Trim and wash the
bell pepper, and cut into
bite-sized pieces. Cut the
bread into cubes. Arrange
the vegetables, bread, and
olives in serving dishes.

3 Grate the hard cheese
coarsely. Cut the soft
cheese into pieces. Peel
and mince the onion and
garlic, then sauté them in
a saucepan with the
remaining 1 tbs oil. Add 1
cup of the stock, the
lemon juice, and oregano
and bring to a boil.

4 Gradually add the
grated cheese to the pot
and cook over low heat,
stirring constantly in a
figure-eight pattern, until
melted. Add the soft
cheese and melt it in the
same manner. With a
hand blender, process the
mixture until smooth.

5 Place the remaining
1/4 cup stock in a small
bowl, add the cornstarch,
and stir until smooth. Add
the cornstarch mixture to
the cheese mixture and
bring to a boil, stirring
constantly. Season with
pepper, and stir in the
parsley. Transfer the
mixture to a preheated
cheese fondue pot, and
place the pot on the table
over the heat source.

6 To eat, spear the
vegetables and bread
with fondue forks and dip
in the cheese.

Cheese-Curry Fondue

● easy
● sophisticated

Serves 4:
10 oz carrots
10 oz celery root (celeriac)
10 oz leeks
7 oz cherry tomatoes
Salt to taste
7 oz sliced roast beef
10 oz cheddar cheese
1 1/4 cups milk
1 tbs cornstarch
1-2 tbs curry powder
10 oz mascarpone cheese
1-2 tbs fresh lemon juice
Pepper to taste

Prep time: 50 minutes
Per serving approx.: 780 calories
/ 37 g protein / 62 g fat / 22 g
carbohydrates

1 Trim, peel, and wash the carrots and celery root. Cut the carrots and celery root into bite-sized pieces. Trim the leeks, wash them well, and cut them into 3/4-inch slices. Wash the tomatoes.

2 Plunge the carrots, celery root, and leeks, one type at a time, into boiling salted water until partially cooked (blanched) about 4 minutes each. Remove the vegetables from the boiling water and place them in a bowl of ice water to cool; drain.

3 Halve the roast beef slices lengthwise, and roll them up loosely. Arrange the roast beef rolls and vegetables on a serving dish.

4 Coarsely grate the cheddar cheese. Place 1/4 cup of the milk in a small bowl or cup, add the cornstarch and curry powder, and stir until smooth. Heat the remaining 1 cup milk in a cheese fondue pot over low heat.

5 Gradually add the grated cheese to the pot and cook over low heat, stirring constantly in a figure-eight pattern, until melted. Stir in dollops of the mascarpone, blending all ingredients until they are smooth.

6 Add the cornstarch mixture to the cheese mixture and bring to a rolling boil, stirring constantly. Stir in the lemon juice and season with pepper. Place the fondue pot on the table over the heat source.

7 To eat, spear the vegetables and beef rolls with fondue forks and dip in the cheese.

Cheese and Herb Fondue

● sophisticated
● easy

Serves 4:
20 oz asparagus
2 bulbs kohlrabi
1/4 cup lemon juice
10 oz peeled cooked
   shrimp
Salt to taste
1 small onion
1 clove garlic
1 tbs butter
1 cup vegetable stock
1/2 cup heavy cream
20 oz cream cheese
4-5 tbs mixed finely
   chopped fresh herbs
Pepper to taste

Prep time: 50 minutes
Per serving approx.: 760 calories
/ 31 g protein / 64 g fat / 20 g
carbohydrates

1 If necessary, peel the bottom third of the asparagus and remove the woody ends. Wash the asparagus and cut it diagonally into 1 1/2-inch pieces. Peel the kohlrabi and cut it into bite-sized cubes. Sprinkle 2 tbs of the lemon juice over the shrimp and set aside.

2 Cook the kohlrabi cubes in boiling salted water until partially cooked (blanched) for about 3 minutes; drain thoroughly. Cook the asparagus in a little boiling salted water for 8-10 minutes, until tender-crisp. Remove the asparagus, plunge it into ice water, and drain the asparagus thoroughly.

3 Arrange the asparagus, kohlrabi, and shrimp on a serving dish.

4 Peel and finely mince the onion and garlic. Melt the butter in a saucepan over medium heat. Add the onion and sauté briefly, until light golden. Stir in the garlic. Add the stock and simmer over low heat for 5 minutes.

5 Add the cream and cream cheese to the pot and cook, stirring constantly in a figure-eight pattern, until you have a smooth, creamy mixture. Mix in the herbs and season the fondue with the remaining 2 tbs lemon juice and pepper. Pour the cheese mixture into a preheated cheese fondue pot and place the pot on the table over the heat source.

6 To eat, spear the vegetables and shrimp on fondue forks and dip in the cheese-herb mixture.

Normandy Fondue

● sophisticated
● vegetarian

Serves 4:
28 oz Camembert cheese
1 large baguette
4-5 small red apples
5 tbs fresh lemon juice
1 clove garlic
1 cup dry hard cider
1/2 cup heavy cream
1/4 cup Calvados, apple
brandy, or apple cider
2 tsp cornstarch
White pepper to taste

Prep time: 40 minutes
Per serving approx.: 1180
calories / 51 g protein / 65 g fat
/ 91 g carbohydrates

1 Remove the rind from the Camembert and cut the cheese into small pieces. Cut the baguette into bite-sized cubes. Wash, dry and quarter the apples, remove the cores, and cut into 8 wedges each. Immediately brush the cut apple surfaces with lemon juice to prevent discoloration. Arrange the bread and apples on a serving dish.

2 Peel the garlic, halve it lengthwise, and vigorously rub the inside of a cheese fondue pot with the cut surfaces. Pour the cider, remaining lemon juice, and cream into the pot and bring to a boil over medium heat.

3 Gradually add the cheese and cook over low heat, stirring constantly in a figure-eight pattern, until you have a thick, creamy mixture.

4 Place the Calvados in a small bowl or cup, add the cornstarch, and stir until smooth. Add the cornstarch mixture to the cheese mixture and bring briefly to a boil, stirring vigorously. Season to taste with pepper. Place the cheese fondue pot on the dining table over the heat source.

5 To eat, spear the bread cubes and apple wedges with fondue forks and dip in the cheese mixture.

above: Normandy Fondue
below: Cheese and Herb
Fondue

Cheese-Walnut Fondue

● inexpensive
● vegetarian

Serves 4:
18 oz tiny boiling potatoes
18 oz carrots
Salt to taste
10 oz Appenzeller cheese
10 oz Gouda cheese
2 oz walnut halves
1 1/4 cups dry white wine
2 tsp cornstarch
2 tsp fresh lemon juice
Pepper to taste
Freshly ground nutmeg
2 tbs chopped fresh chives

Prep time: 45 minutes
Per serving approx.: 750 calories
/ 40 g protein / 45 g fat / 34 g
carbohydrates

1 Scrub the potatoes well, and leave the peels on. Depending on their size, boil them for 15-20 minutes, until they are just barely cooked.

2 Meanwhile, peel the carrots, rinse them, and cut them diagonally into 3/4-inch slices. Cook the carrots in boiling salted water for 5 minutes; they should still be crunchy. Plunge the carrots into cold water and drain them thoroughly.

3 Peel the potatoes, or leave the peels on, as desired, and keep them warm in a low oven. Arrange the carrots and potatoes on a platter.

4 Remove the rinds from the cheeses, and grate them coarsely. Chop the walnuts coarsely. Place 1/4 cup of the white wine in a small bowl or cup. Add the cornstarch, and stir until smooth. Bring the remaining 1 cup wine and the lemon juice to a boil in a cheese fondue pot. Gradually add the cheeses and cook over low heat, stirring constantly in a figure-eight pattern, until you have a thick, creamy mixture.

5 Add the cornstarch mixture to the cheese mixture and bring briefly to a boil, stirring constantly. Stir in the nuts and season to taste with pepper and nutmeg. Sprinkle the chives over the top. Place the fondue pot on the table over the heat source.

6 To eat, spear the potatoes and carrots with fondue forks and dip in the cheese-nut mixture.

Variations
Try this fondue with hazelnuts and use different types of bread instead of potatoes.

Mushroom-Cheese Fondue

● sophisticated
● vegetarian

Serves 4:
6 stalks celery
8 oz tiny white mushrooms
6 small tomatoes
2 firm, ripe pears
2 tbs fresh lemon juice
14 oz walnut bread
1 clove garlic
18 oz Gorgonzola cheese
(or Roquefort, Castello
Blue or Bleu d'Auvergne)
About 1 1/4 cups milk
8 oz cream cheese
3 tsp cornstarch
Pepper to taste

Prep time: 45 minutes
Per serving approx.: 1040
calories / 42 g protein / 65 g fat
/ 77 g carbohydrates

1 Trim the celery, wash, pat dry, and cut it diagonally into 1 1/4-inch pieces. If necessary, rinse the mushrooms briefly and pat dry. Trim the mushroom stems.

2 Wash and dry the tomatoes and pears. Quarter the tomatoes and remove the cores. Quarter the unpeeled pears, remove the cores, and cut them into 16 wedges. Immediately brush the cut pear surfaces with lemon juice to prevent them from turning brown

3 Cut the walnut bread into finger-width slices, then into bite-sized chunks. Arrange the bread in a basket. Arrange the celery, mushrooms, tomatoes, and pears on a serving dish.

4 Peel the garlic, halve it lengthwise, and vigorously rub the inside of a cheese fondue pot with the cut surfaces. Remove the rind from the cheese. Break or cut the cheese into small chunks.

5 Pour 1 cup of the milk into the fondue pot, and heat over low heat. Gradually add the cheese and cook, stirring constantly in a figure-eight pattern, until melted. Gradually add the cream cheese, stirring constantly. Using a hand blender, mix all ingredients until a smooth mixture forms. Add a little more milk if necessary.

6 Place the remaining 1/4 cup milk in a small bowl or cup, add the cornstarch, and stir until smooth. Add the cornstarch mixture to the cheese mixture and bring the fondue to a rolling boil, stirring constantly. Season the fondue with pepper and place the fondue pot on the table over the heat source.

7 To eat, spear the vegetables, pears, mushrooms, and bread with fondue forks and dip in the cheese mixture.

Variations

Instead of celery, serve raw fennel. In place of pears, serve firm, tart apples.

Tip! If you can't find walnut bread, try a hearty sunflower or pumpkin-seed bread.

above: Mushroom–Cheese Fondue
below: Cheese–Walnut Fondue

There's nothing as festive as a fondue party—sitting around a sizzling pot encircled by all kinds of delicious sauces and dips. Best of all, even the host can have fun because everything can be prepared ahead of time. Every diner becomes their own personal chef as they cook whatever catches their fancy.

The Heat Source

A good heat source is needed for all types of fondue. A warmer fueled by tea lights is unsuitable (except in the case the heat-sensitive chocolate fondue) because it doesn't get hot enough. Modern fondue pots contain a replaceable aluminum container that can be filled with sterno, which is easier to handle, less hazardous to use, and has less of an odor than old-fashioned alcohol burners. As an alternative, you can use electric hotplates and electric fondue pots, which allow you to adjust the temperature depending on the type of fondue you are making. For example, a cheese fondue should be kept at 185°F, a stock fondue at 212°F, and an oil fondue at 350°F.

The Fondue Pot

An oil fondue requires a high temperature and, therefore, a pot made of a highly conductive material, such as cast-iron, stainless steel, or copper. The pot should narrow slightly at the top to prevent the oil or broth from spattering. For an oil fondue, it is wise to use a special spatter guard that simultaneously serves as a fork holder (see photo, page 17). Be sure to read the manufacturer's instructions thoroughly before using a fondue pot.

Oil Fondues

Practical Accessories

Fondue forks are long and have 1-2 thin tines at the end. Ideally, the forks should be color-coded so that each diner can retrieve his or her own personal tidbit after it has finished cooking. Fondue forks are used only for cooking, so the diner won't burn his or her mouth after cooking the morsel; the food is eaten with regular silverware after being removed from the fondue fork. Provide 1-2 fondue forks for each person. A wide variety of fondue plates can be found in housewares stores. Most are divided into sections for meat, fish, vegetables, and sauces, but you can also use regular dinner plates.

The Right Oil

Fondue oils must be heated to 350°F, because, especially in the case of meat, this temperature causes the food's pores to close quickly so that no juice can escape and no oil can penetrate. The most suitable oils are those you would use for deep-frying—odorless and flavorless vegetable-based oils such as sunflower oil, peanut oil, canola oil, or soybean oil. Butter, margarine, and cold-pressed oils should not be used for fondue, as they have very low smoke points. Fill the fondue pot halfway with oil, cover, and let it heat. To test the oil's temperature, insert the handle of a wooden spoon into the oil. If you see small bubbles forming around the handle, the oil is ready for cooking.

After the meal, when the oil has completely cooled, pour it through a paper coffee filter and store it in a cool, dark place. If strained properly, you can reuse the oil 1-2 times for a fondue or for deep-frying. When you dispose of oil, don't pour it down the drain. Instead, discard it in a proper container—an empty cardboard milk carton or used coffee tin are good choices.

Quality Ingredients

Whether you're cooking meat, poultry, fish, vegetables, or fruits, be sure to use top-quality ingredients. For beef, choose fillets, loin cuts, rump, and any type of steak. For pork, choose tenderloin or cutlets. For poultry, use boneless breast meat. For seafood, choose fish fillets or peeled shrimp. Vegetables and fruits should be fresh, ripe, and free of holes or other blemishes.

Basic fondue equipment: Fondue pot with spatter guard and suitable heat source, fondue forks, sectioned plates, and small bowls for the sauces

Tips and Tricks

• To prevent the hot oil from spattering when you dip the ingredients into it, thoroughly pat dry all fondue ingredients and do not season them ahead of time.
• Never put too many forks into the hot oil at once, as this lowers the temperature too quickly and the ingredients cannot cook properly.
• Never leave the hot fondue pot or the lit heat source unattended. Be extremely cautious, especially if children are present at the table.

Meatball Fondue

● easy
● can prepare in advance

Serves 4:
Meatballs:
1 green onion
1 small red chile
1 tbs pine nuts
14 oz ground beef or lamb
2 eggs
Grated zest and juice from
  1 lemon
1 tsp dried oregano
2-4 tbs bread crumbs
Salt & pepper to taste
14 oz bulk sausage
1 tbs golden raisins
2 tbs chopped fresh Italian
  parsley
Mint Sauce:
1/4 cucumber
1/2 bunch fresh dill
3 sprigs fresh mint
1-2 cloves garlic
8 oz plain yogurt
1 tbs white wine vinegar
Salt & pepper to taste

Tomato-Curry Sauce, p 22
6 quarts vegetable oil

Prep time: 1 1/4 hours
Per serving approx.: 1050
calories / 37 g protein / 37 g fat
/ 45 g carbohydrates

1 Trim and wash the
green onion and chile.
Remove the seeds from
the chile and finely chop
both ingredients. Coarsely
chop the pine nuts.

2 For the beef or lamb
meatballs, mix together
the ground beef or lamb,
green onion, 1 of the
eggs, the lemon zest,

lemon juice, oregano, and
1-2 tbs of the bread
crumbs. Season with salt
and pepper.

3 For the sausage
meatballs, mix together
the sausage, raisins, chile,
pine nuts, parsley,
remaining 1 egg, and 1-2
tbs bread crumbs. Season
with salt and pepper.

4 From the two types of
meat mixtures, form
walnut-sized balls and
arrange on a serving dish.

5 For the mint sauce:
Peel the cucumber, halve
it lengthwise, remove the
seeds, and grate the flesh
coarsely. Wash, shake dry,
and chop the herbs. Peel
and mince the garlic. In a
bowl, mix the yogurt with
the vinegar, cucumber,
and herbs. Stir in the
garlic. Season with salt
and pepper.

6 Pour the curry sauce
into a serving bowl.

7 Heat the oil in the
fondue pot to 350°F and
place it on the table over
the heat source. To eat,
place the meatballs in
wire ladles and fry until
cooked through. Serve
with the dipping sauces.

Tex-Mex Fondue

● can prepare in advance
● sophisticated

Serves 4:
14 oz boneless beef rump
14 oz boneless turkey
  breast
3 small onions
5 cloves garlic
1 bunch fresh thyme
6 cups vegetable oil
Pineapple-Carrot Salad:
3 carrots
1 fresh pineapple (about
  28 oz)
1 small onion
1-2 fresh red chiles
1/4 cup vegetable oil
1 tsp sugar
Juice from 2 oranges
Juice from 1 lemon
Salt & pepper to taste
Mole Negro:
2-4 dried red chiles
1 tbs sesame seeds
1 small onion
2 cloves garlic
About 2 oz tortilla or
  potato chips
2 tbs roasted peanuts
1/4 cup vegetable
  shortening (or lard)
1 1/2 oz unsweetened
  chocolate
1/2 cup chicken stock
Dash of ground cinnamon

1 cup purchased guacamole

Prep time: 1 3/4 hours
Marinating time: Overnight
Per serving approx.: 1040
calories / 52 g protein / 67 g fat
/ 66 g carbohydrates

1 The day before you
plan to eat, cut the beef
and turkey into thin
slices, then into strips.

Peel the onions and 3
cloves of the garlic. Cut
the onions into rings.
Slice the garlic. Wash and
shake dry the thyme. In a
bowl, mix the above
ingredients with 1 cup of
the oil. Cover the bowl
and marinate overnight in
the refrigerator.

2 For the salad: peel the
carrots and slice them
thinly. Cut the pineapple
into eighths, remove the
core, cut off the skin, and
slice the fruit. Peel and
dice the onion. Trim the
chiles, cut them in half
lengthwise, rinse out the
seeds, and cut the flesh
into strips. In a skillet,
heat the oil over medium
heat. Add the carrots,
onion, chiles, and sugar,
and sauté for 1 minute.
Add the orange and
lemon juices. Add the
pineapple and simmer,
covered, for 5 minutes,
until the vegetables are
tender. Season with salt
and pepper.

3 For the mole negro:
Trim the chiles, cut them
in half lengthwise, remove
the seeds (reserving
them), and chop the flesh.
In a dry skillet, lightly
toast the chile seeds and

sesame seeds until lightly browned and aromatic. Peel and dice the onion and garlic. Crush the chips and nuts. In a skillet, heat the shortening over medium heat until melted. Add the chiles, seeds, onion, garlic, chips, and nuts, and sauté for 5 minutes. Remove the skillet from the heat, and stir in pieces of the chocolate until melted. Add the stock, and puree the mixture with a hand blender or in a regular blender. Season with the ground cinnamon.

5 Remove the meat from the marinade and pat it dry. Peel the remaining 2 garlic cloves. Heat the garlic in the fondue pot with remaining 5 cups oil to 350°F and place the pot on the table over the heat source; remove the garlic cloves (take care that they do not burn). Heat up the mole negro, skimming any fat that forms on the surface. To eat, spear the meat with fondue forks and fry in the oil until cooked through. Accompany with the salad, mole negro, and guacamole.

above: Meatball Fondue
below: Tex-Mex Fondue

Traditional Meat Fondue (Fondue Bourguignonne)

● easy
● sophisticated

Serves 4:

Mustard Dipping Sauce:
1 1/4 cups light
  mayonnaise
2 tbs sour cream
4 tsp Dijon-style mustard
1-2 tbs fresh lemon juice
Salt & pepper to taste
1 tbs chopped fresh chives

Green Peppercorn Sauce:
1/2 cup crème fraîche
3 tbs sour cream
3 tbs ketchup
1 tbs green peppercorns
1 tbs brandy (optional)
Salt to taste
Several drops of Tabasco
  sauce

Curry-Banana Sauce:
1 ripe banana
1/2 cup light mayonnaise
1/2 cup plain yogurt
1-2 tbs mild curry powder
2 tbs fresh lemon juice
Salt & pepper to taste
A few fresh mint leaves

28 oz beef fillet
1 small jar (about 6 oz)
  cornichons (gherkins)
1 small jar (about 6 oz)
  pickled vegetables
1 small jar (about 6 oz)
  cocktail onions
6 cups vegetable oil
Salt & pepper to taste

Prep time: 40 minutes
Per serving approx.: 1020
calories / 40 g protein / 84 g fat
/ 24 g carbohydrates

1 For the mustard sauce: Stir together the mayonnaise, sour cream, mustard, and lemon juice until creamy. Season with salt and pepper, and sprinkle with the chives.

2 For the green peppercorn sauce: Stir all of the ingredients together well.

3 For the curry-banana sauce: Peel the banana, place it in a bowl, and mash it with a fork. Stir in the mayonnaise, yogurt, curry (to taste), and lemon juice. Season with salt and pepper. Sprinkle with the mint.

4 Cut the meat into 1 1/4-inch cubes and arrange them on a serving dish. Drain the cornichons, pickled vegetables, and cocktail onions separately, and pour them into small serving bowls. Heat the oil in fondue pot to 350°F and place it on the table over the heat source.

5 To eat, spear the beef with fondue forks and fry in the oil until cooked through. Season with salt and pepper and dip into the sauces. Accompany with the pickles and pickled vegetables.

Poultry Fondue with Artichokes

- inexpensive
- easy

Serves 4:

14 oz boneless, skinless chicken or turkey breast
9 oz chicken or turkey livers (or substitute more chicken or turkey breast)
Pepper to taste
1/4 cup dry sherry
Chive Vinaigrette:
1 tomato
2 oz pitted green olives
1 bunch fresh chives
1/2 cup fresh lemon juice
Salt & white pepper to taste
1/2 tsp mustard
5 tbs olive oil
5 tbs sunflower oil
1/2 cup vegetable stock

1 jar artichoke hearts (7 oz), drained
6 oz sliced bacon
6 cups vegetable oil

Prep time: 40 minutes
Per serving approx.: 850 calories / 49 g protein / 63 g fat / 17 g carbohydrates

1 Cut the poultry breast into bite-sized cubes. Rinse the livers, pat dry, and cut them into bite-sized chunks. In separate bowls, mix the poultry and livers with pepper and 2 tbs of the sherry. Cover the bowl and re-frigerate until serving.

2 For the vinaigrette: Cut an X into the round end of the tomato and plunge it into boiling water to loosen the skin. With a paring knife, pull off the tomato skin. Cut the tomato in half, squeeze out the seeds, and finely chop the flesh. Finely chop the olives. Wash, shake dry, and chop the chives. In a bowl, stir the lemon juice, salt, pepper and mustard. While whisking, drizzle in the oils and stock. Stir in the tomato, olives, and chives.

3 Quarter the artichoke hearts and sprinkle with pepper. Halve the bacon slices crosswise.

4 Wrap a bacon slice around each artichoke quarter and spear with a toothpick. Remove the meat from the marinade, pat dry, and arrange on a serving dish with the wrapped artichokes.

5 Heat the oil in the fondue pot to 350°F and place it on the table over the heat source. To eat, spear the ingredients with fondue forks, fry them in the hot oil until cooked through and dip in the chive vinaigrette

Potato Fondue

● inexpensive
● can prepare in advance

Serves 4:
2 1/4 lb large Yukon gold
   potatoes
About 1 lb small boiling
   potatoes
2 tbs caraway seeds
Salt to taste
Tomato-Curry Sauce:
1 clove garlic
1 tbs canola oil
1 tbs curry powder
1 can tomato puree
   (15 oz)
1/2 cup vegetable stock

Salt & pepper to taste
1 jar pickled vegetables
   (12 oz)
8 oz shallots
10 oz bacon (unsliced)
6 cups vegetable oil

Prep time: 40 minutes
Per serving approx.: 995 calories
/ 35 g protein / 61 g fat / 83 g
carbohydrates

1 Scrub all of the
potatoes well. Boil the
large potatoes in salted
water with the caraway
seeds until they are
slightly undercooked,
about 15-18 minutes. Boil
the small potatoes in
salted water for about 15
minutes, until just cooked.

2 For the tomato-curry
sauce: Peel and finely
chop the garlic. In a
skillet, heat the oil over
medium heat. Add the
garlic and sauté briefly.

Stir in the curry powder
and sauté briefly. Stir in
the tomato puree and
vegetable stock. Reduce
the heat to low and
simmer the mixture until
it thickens to a dip
consistency. Season with
salt and pepper.

3 Put the tomato-curry
sauce and pickled
vegetables in separate
serving bowls.

4 If desired, peel the
potatoes. Leave the small
potatoes whole. Cut the
large potatoes into thick
strips, cubes, or slices.

5 Peel the shallots, halve
larger shallots lengthwise,
and leave smaller shallots
whole. Cut the bacon into
1 1/2-inch pieces.
Arrange all of the ingredients in serving dishes.

6 Heat the oil in a
fondue pot to 350°F and
place it on the table over
the heat source. To eat,
spear the ingredients with
fondue forks and fry them
in the oil until cooked
through. Accompany with
the dipping sauce and
pickled vegetables.

Rustic Meat Fondue

● inexpensive
● easy

Serves 4:
1 onion
6 cups vegetable oil
1 tsp dried oregano
2 oz roasted red bell
   peppers (from a jar)
18 oz ground beef
2 egg yolks
1 tsp capers
About 2 cups bread
   crumbs
Salt to taste
Tabasco sauce to taste
5 oz pickles
10 oz roast pork, thinly
   sliced
2 tbs mustard
Flour
2 eggs, beaten
Sweet Corn Sauce:
1 can sweet corn kernels
   (7 oz), drained
2/3 cup light mayonnaise
1/2 cup buttermilk
1 tbs chopped fresh Italian
   parsley
Salt to taste
Worcestershire sauce to
   taste
Cayenne pepper to taste
Fresh lemon juice to taste
Cucumber Salad:
1/2 cucumber
8 hard-boiled eggs
1 red bell pepper
About 1 bunch mixed fresh
   herbs
5 tbs white wine vinegar
Salt to taste
1 tsp mustard
8 tbs sunflower oil

Prep time: 1 hour
Marinating time: 30 minutes
Per serving approx.: 1510
calories / 44 g protein / 87 g fat
/ 155 g carbohydrates

1 Peel and dice the
onion. In a skillet, heat 2
tbs of the oil over
medium heat. Add the
onion and oregano and
sauté until translucent.
Chop the bell peppers. In
a bowl, mix the onion
mixture, peppers, ground
beef, egg yolks, capers,
and 3-5 tbs of the bread
crumbs. Season with salt
and Tabasco, form the
mixture into walnut-sized
balls, and place on a
serving dish.

2 Quarter the pickles
lengthwise. Spread the
meat slices with the
mustard, place a pickle
quarter on each slice, and
roll up securely. In
separate shallow bowls,
place the flour, eggs, and
the remaining bread
crumbs. Dredge the meat
rolls first in the flour,
then in the eggs, then in
the bread crumbs.
Arrange the rolls on a
serving dish.

3 For the corn sauce:
With a hand blender or in
a regular blender, puree
half of the corn with the
mayonnaise and
buttermilk. Stir in the
remaining corn and the

parsley. Season with salt, Worcestershire, cayenne, and lemon juice.

4 For the cucumber salad: Peel the cucumber, halve it lengthwise, remove the seeds with a spoon, and cut the flesh into slices. Peel the eggs and cut them lengthwise into eighths. Trim, wash, and dice the red bell pepper. Wash, shake dry, and chop the herbs, and mix them in a large bowl with the vinegar, salt, mustard, and oil. Stir in the cucumber, bell pepper, and eggs. Cover the bowl and refrigerate the salad for 30 minutes.

5 Heat the remaining oil in a fondue pot to 350°F and place it on the table over the heat source. To eat, place the meatballs and meat rolls in wire ladles and fry them in the oil until cooked through. Accompany with the corn sauce and salad.

above: Potato Fondue
below: Rustic Meat Fondue

Duck Fondue

- sophisticated
- can prepare in advance

Serves 4:
24 oz boneless duck breast
2 cloves garlic
1 piece fresh ginger, about
   1 1/4 inches long
1/2 cup soy sauce
3 tbs sherry vinegar
1/4 cup prune juice

Vegetable Pickles:
1 cucumber
1 small daikon radish
2 tsp salt
1 carrot
1–2 red chiles
6 tbs cider vinegar
6 tbs apple juice
1 tbs sugar

Peanut Sauce:
2 cloves garlic
1 piece fresh ginger, about
   1/3-inch long
1 stalk lemon grass
4 oz roasted peanuts
3 tbs soy sauce
1 tsp brown sugar
1 can unsweetened
   coconut milk (14 oz)

6 cups vegetable oil
1 cup purchased plum
   sauce

Prep time: 1 hour
Marinating time: 3 hours
Per serving approx.: 805 calories
/ 44 g protein / 50 g fat / 48 g
carbohydrates

1 Slice the duck thinly. Peel and slice the garlic and ginger. In a bowl, mix the ginger, garlic, soy sauce, vinegar, and prune juice. Add the duck , toss well, cover the bowl, and refrigerator for 3 hours.

2 For the pickles: Peel the cucumber and radish, slice them thinly, and place them in a colander inside a bowl. Sprinkle the vegetables with the salt, fill the bowl with water, and soak for 1 hour. Peel the carrot and cut it into thin strips. Cut the chiles in half length-wise, rinse out the seeds, and chop the flesh. In a saucepan, bring the carrot and chiles to a boil with the vinegar, juice, and sugar. While still hot, mix in the drained cucumber and radish, and marinate for 2 hours.

3 For the peanut sauce: Peel the garlic and ginger and trim the lemon grass. Chop the garlic, ginger, and lemon grass, and place in a bowl or blender. With a hand blender or regular blender, puree the mixture with the remaining ingredients.

4 Heat the oil in a fondue pot to 350°F and place on the table over the heat source. Pat dry the duck and arrange on a serving platter. To eat, spear the duck on fondue forks and fry until cooked through. Accompany with the vegetable pickles and dipping sauces.

Crunchy Vegetable Fondue

● inexpensive
● vegetarian

Serves 4:

Batter:
2 cups flour
2 eggs
Grated zest of 1 lemon
Salt & pepper to taste
Freshly grated nutmeg to taste
1 can beer (12 oz)

Creamy Herb Sauce:
About 2 bunches mixed fresh herbs
1/2 bunch radishes
2 cups crème fraîche
3 tbs plain yogurt
1 tsp mustard
2 tbs fresh lemon juice
Salt & pepper to taste

3 1/2 lb mixed fresh vegetables (such as broccoli, cauliflower, bell peppers, zucchini, and carrots)
6 cups vegetable oil

Prep time: 1 1/4 hours
Per serving approx.: 830 calories / 19 g protein / 47 g fat / 87 g carbohydrates

1 For the batter: Mix the flour, eggs, lemon zest, pinch of salt, dash of pepper, nutmeg, and beer in a bowl until smooth. Cover the bowl and set it aside until serving time.

2 For the herb sauce: Wash the herbs, shake dry, and chop them very finely. Trim the radishes, wash well, and finely grate them. In a bowl, mix the herbs and radishes with the crème fraîche, yogurt, and mustard. Stir in the lemon juice and season with salt and pepper.

3 Trim, wash, and, if necessary, peel the vegetables. Cut the vegetables into bite-sized chunks. Cook harder vegetables, such as broccoli, cauliflower, and carrots, in boiling, salted water for 4–5 minutes; they should remain crunchy. Plunge the partially cooked vegetables into cold water to stop the cooking and drain thoroughly.

4 Distribute the batter among 4 small bowls. Arrange the vegetables on a serving platter. Heat the oil in a fondue pot to 350°F and place on the table over the heat source.

5 To eat, pierce the vegetables with fondue forks, dip them in the batter, and let excess batter drip off. Fry the vegetables in the hot oil until golden brown. Accompany with the herb sauce.

Chips & Dips

● easy
● can prepare in advance

Serves 4:
18 oz potatoes
18 oz root vegetables
(such as carrots, celery
root, turnips)
Salt to taste
Goat Cheese Dip:
1 bunch fresh basil
1 log soft goat cheese
(about 5-6 oz)
2 oz Parmesan cheese,
grated
1/4 cup sour cream
1/4 cup butter, softened
Salt & pepper to taste
Creamy Mushroom Dip
8 oz white mushrooms
1 clove garlic
1 tbs vegetable oil
1/4 cup dry sherry or stock
1 cup heavy cream
2 oz diced tomatoes
1 tbs chopped fresh Italian
parsley
Salt, pepper, & sugar to
taste
6 cups vegetable oil
Purchased chili sauce

Prep time: 1 hour
Per serving approx.: 850 calories
/ 29 g protein / 64 g fat / 40 g
carbohydrates

1 Trim, peel, and rinse
the potatoes and root
vegetables, then cut them
into thin slices. Plunge
the potatoes and
vegetables into boiling
salted water for 2
minutes. Drain well, then
plunge them into cold
water, drain well again,
and pat dry thoroughly.

2 For the goat cheese
dip: Wash, shake dry, and
chop the basil. Remove
the rind from the cheese
and mash it in a bowl
with the basil, Parmesan,
sour cream, and butter.
Season the dip with salt
and pepper.

3 For the creamy
mushroom dip: Wipe
clean the mushrooms and
peel the garlic. Chop the
mushrooms and garlic. In
a skillet, heat the oil over
medium-high heat. Add
the mushrooms and garlic
and sauté briefly. Add the
sherry, cover, and cook for
1 minute. Stir in the
cream and diced
tomatoes, and simmer
over low heat until the
sauce is thick and creamy.
Stir in the parsley and
season with salt, pepper,
and sugar.

4 Heat the oil in fondue
pot to 350°F and place on
the table over the heat
source. To eat, place the
potatoes and vegetables
in a wire ladle and fry in
the hot oil until crisp.
Season the chips lightly
with salt and accompany
with the dips and sauce.

Mussel Fondue

● can prepare in advance
● takes a while

Serves 6:
5 lb black mussels
1/2 cup dry white wine
1 bunch fresh sage
9 oz sliced bacon
Golden Raisin Sauce:
1/4 cup golden raisins
5 tbs brandy or water
1 cup ketchup
2 tbs currant jelly
2 tbs grape juice
1/2 tsp Worcestershire
sauce
1 tsp horseradish
Olive-Almond Sauce:
8 anchovies
1/2 cup milk
4 oz pitted green olives
4 oz pitted black olives
1 clove garlic
1 bunch fresh chives
3 tbs finely chopped
almonds
3 tbs extra-virgin olive oil
Pepper & sugar to taste
Lemon-Thyme Mayonnaise:
1 lemon
6 sprigs lemon thyme
1 1/2 cups mayonnaise
Salt, pepper, & sugar to
taste
6 cups vegetable oil

Prep time: 1 1/2 hours
Per serving approx.: 925 calories
/ 38 g protein / 70 g fat / 32 g
carbohydrates

1 Rinse the mussels
thoroughly and remove
any hairy filaments
(beards). Discard any
open mussels. In a large
pot, heat the wine until
very hot and add the

mussels. Cover the pot
and cook the mussels
until almost all have
opened, about 3-5
minutes, stirring often.

2 Remove the pot from
the heat and discard any
mussel shells that are still
closed. Let the mussels
cool, then remove them
from the shell. Wash and
shake dry the sage, then
pick off the leaves. Cut
the bacon into 2-inch
pieces and lay them on a
work surface. On each
piece of bacon, place 1
sage leaf and 1 mussel.
Roll up the bacon around
the mussel and secure the
rolls with toothpicks.

3 For the golden raisin
sauce: Put the golden
raisins in a saucepan with
the brandy and bring to a
boil. Remove from the
heat. When cool, stir in
the remaining ingredients.

4 For the olive-almond
sauce: Soak the anchovies
in the milk for 30
minutes; drain, discarding
the milk. Chop the
anchovies with the olives
and peeled garlic. Wash,
shake dry, and chop the
chives. Mix all the
ingredients together with

the almonds and oil, seasoning with pepper and sugar.

5 For the lemon-thyme mayonnaise: Grate the zest from 1/4 of the lemon and place in a bowl. Squeeze the juice from the lemon into the bowl. Wash and shake dry the thyme, and chop the leaves and add to the bowl. Stir in the mayonnaise and season with salt, pepper, and sugar.

6 Heat the oil in a fondue pot to 350°F and place on the table over the heat source. To eat, pierce the mussel rolls with fondue forks and fry them in the oil until the bacon is crisp. Accompany with the dipping sauces.

above: Chips & Dips
below: Mussel Fondue

S tock fondues, which originated in Asia, are fondues in which the ingredients are cooked in stock instead of oil. This type of fondue is steadily gaining in popularity in our part of the world because it unites simple, healthy cooking with interesting, ethnic flavors. Stock fondues can be prepared in a meat fondue pot, in a saucepan, or in a small wok. If you want to be truly authentic, you can serve it in a hot pot (see page 40).

The Importance of Chopping

To ensure quick, even cooking, the ingredients for a stock fondue should be chopped as finely as possible.

To make thin strips and cubes: first cut meat, fish, and vegetables into thin slices, then stack the slices and cut them into thin strips. If desired, you can then cut the strips into cubes.

To ease cutting meat, wrap it well and place it in the freezer for about 1 hour. This will make the meat firm for cutting even pieces.

For vegetables, the following general rule applies: When the vegetable has a soft texture (for example, mushrooms, snow peas, leeks, and green onions), the pieces should be left large. When the vegetable has a firm texture (for example, carrots, celery root, broccoli, cauliflower, Brussels sprouts, and beans), the pieces need to be cut smaller and may need to be partially cooked (blanched).

Stock Fondues

Basic Stock

If you have the time and the inclination, it's worth making your stock for fondue from scratch. You can even prepare it ahead of time and freeze it. If you're in a hurry, use good-quality, low-sodium stock from a can. The stock must be light so that the ingredients retain their unique flavor when cooked. While you're cooking the fondue, the stock will become so hearty that you can enjoy it afterwards as a light soup.

Basic Chicken Stock

To a large pot, add a large roasting chicken, about 2 quarts of water (to cover the chicken), 1 roughly chopped carrot, 1 roughly chopped leek, 1 peeled and quartered onion, a couple sprigs fresh Italian parsley, 1 bay leaf, and 5 peppercorns. Bring the water to a boil, remove the scum on the surface, and simmer, covered, for 1 1/2 hours over low heat. Pour the stock through a sieve, season sparingly with salt and pepper, and cool completely. (Use the cooked chicken for another dish, such as pulled from the bone for a chicken salad.) When cool, skim the fat from the surface of the stock. Makes about 6 cups.

Basic Meat Stock: Instead of a chicken, use 3-4 marrow bones and 1 1/4 pounds of beef stew meat. Simmer the meat very gently for no more than 2 hours. Makes about 6 cups.

A Brief Guide to Quantities

If you're planning to serve fondue to a greater or lesser number of people than is specified in a recipe, here are a some guidelines for shopping. For each person, plan on:
• 6 to 8 oz of the main item, such as meat, poultry, or fish
• 8 oz of vegetables (for a vegetarian fondue, figure 10-14 oz of vegetables)
• A total of 1/2 cup sauce per person
• About 4 oz per person bread for accompaniment

Tips and Tricks

• Avoid seasoning the ingredients before cooking, or the stock will be too strongly flavored to sip at the end.
• Be sure that the stock continues to simmer slightly in the pot throughout the meal.
• Don't hesitate to combine meat, fish, and vegetables in one fondue.
• For any ingredients that can't be speared on a fondue fork, wire ladles are a super tool. These small, long-handled, metal sieves are available in Asian markets or kitchenware stores.

Homemade chicken stock: Vegetables, herbs, and spices give it a nice flavor and aroma

Fish Fondue

● low-cal
● sophisticated

Serves 4-6:
7 oz fresh spinach
Salt to taste
Cranberry-Horseradish Sauce:
1/4 cup creamy-style horseradish
3 tbs plain yogurt
1/4 cup whole-berry cranberry sauce
1 tbs lemon juice
Salt & pepper to taste
Almond-Garlic Sauce:
2-3 cloves garlic
4 oz skinned almonds
6 tbs vegetable stock
2 tbs vegetable oil
1-2 tbs fresh lemon juice
Salt to taste

10 oz cod fillet
Lemon pepper seasoning to taste
10 oz salmon fillet
10 oz halibut fillet
3 tbs fresh lemon juice
1 quart fish or vegetable stock
1 cup water
1/8 tsp ground saffron
2 tbs fresh dill leaves

Prep time: 1 hour
Per serving approx.: 370 calories / 35 g protein / 18 g fat / 11 g carbohydrates

1 Wash the spinach and pull off the stems. Put the leaves in a large skillet, season lightly with salt, and place over medium heat until just wilted.

2 For the cranberry-horseradish sauce: Mix together the horseradish, yogurt, 3 tbs of the cranberry sauce, and the lemon juice. Season with salt and pepper. Transfer the sauce to a serving dish and garnish the top with the remaining 1 tbs cranberry sauce.

3 For the almond-garlic sauce: peel the garlic and puree it with the almonds. Stir in the stock and oil. Stir in the lemon juice, and season with salt.

4 Cut the cod into large cubes and season with salt and lemon pepper. On a work surface, overlap 2-3 spinach leaves. Place a cod cube on the leaves and wrap them around the fish to form a small package. Repeat with the remaining spinach and cod. Cut the salmon into strips, and cut the halibut into large cubes. Drizzle the lemon juice over the fish. Arrange the ingredients on serving dishes.

5 Bring the stock and water to a boil in a fondue pot and place over the heat source. Dissolve the saffron in the stock and add the dill. To eat, put the fish in wire ladles and cook it in the stock. Accompany with the dipping sauces.

Curried Seafood Fondue

● sophisticated
○ takes a while

Serves 4:
Fruited Rice Salad:
2 fresh red chiles
1/2 cup canola oil
4 oz frozen peas
1 tsp sugar
3/4 cup long-grain rice
1 cup fish stock
1/2 cup dry white wine or stock
1 ripe mango
1/4 fresh pineapple, peeled
Juice of 2 limes
5 tbs fruit juice
Salt, pepper, & sugar to taste

3 cloves garlic
Juice and grated zest from 4 limes
20 large shrimp, peeled
10 sea scallops, side muscles removed
4 mild, white fish fillets
1 piece fresh ginger (about 1 inch)
1 stalk lemon grass
1 can unsweetened coconut milk (14 oz)
3 tbs yellow curry paste
2 1/2 cups fish stock
2 bunches fresh basil

Prep. time: 1 3/4 hours
Marinating time: 2 hours
Per serving approx.: 1020 calories / 81 g protein / 34 g fat / 90 g carbohydrates

1 For the rice salad: Trim the chiles, cut them in half lengthwise, rinse out the seeds and cut the flesh into strips. In a saucepan, heat 2 tbs of the oil over medium heat. Stir in the peas, sugar, and rice, and sauté until translucent. Add the stock and wine. Cover the pan, reduce the heat to low, and cook for about 15 minutes, until holes form on the surface of the rice. Turn off the heat and let the rice stand for 10 minutes. Let the rice cool. Peel the mango, cut flesh from the pit, and cut the flesh into cubes. Remove the core of the pineapple and cut the flesh into cubes. In a large bowl, mix the lime juice and fruit juice with the remaining 6 tbs oil and season with salt, pepper, and sugar. Stir in the rice and fruits, cover the bowl, and marinate for 2 hours.

2 Peel and chop the garlic. In a medium bowl, mix 1/3 of the garlic with half each of the lime juice and zest. Rinse the shrimp, scallops, and fish fillets, and pat dry. Cut the scallops in half through the diameter. Cut the fish into 1 1/2-inch pieces. Add the fish and seafood to the bowl with the marinade toss to coat well. Cover the bowl and refrigerate for 1 hour.

3 Peel the ginger and trim the lemon grass. Finely chop the ginger and the lower third of the lemon grass. Remove the thick cap from the coconut milk, and add the cap to a saucepan with the ginger, lemon grass, remaining garlic, remaining lime zest, and the curry paste. Simmer for 3 minutes over low heat, stirring constantly. Add the coconut milk, remaining lime juice, and fish stock, and simmer for 5 minutes; cool.

4 Wash and shake dry the basil, then remove the leaves from the stalks. Thoroughly drain the seafood mixture. Thread the seafood onto wooden skewers, alternating types and placing a basil leaf between each piece. Place the curry stock in a fondue pot, bring to a boil, and place on the table over the heat source. To eat, place the seafood skewers in the curry broth until cooked through. Retrieve the skewers with wire ladles. Accompany with the fruited rice salad.

above: Fish Fondue; below: Curried Seafood Fondue

Chile-Spiked Pork Fondue

● low-cal
● easy

Serves 4:
20 oz pork tenderloin
9 oz Chinese cabbage
9 oz carrots
4 fresh red chiles
1 inch fresh ginger
Sweet-Sour Sauce:
1 green onion
2 cloves garlic
3/4 inch fresh ginger
2 tbs sesame oil
3/4 cup chicken stock
6 tbs ketchup
1/2 cup rice vinegar
1/4 cup sugar
1 1/2 tsp cornstarch
2 tbs water
Salt & pepper to taste
6 cups light meat stock
5 tbs light soy sauce

Prep time: 40 minutes
Freezing time: 1 hour
Per serving approx.: 490 calories
/ 28 g protein / 27 g fat / 37 g
carbohydrates

1 Wrap the pork in plastic wrap and freeze for about 1 hour.

2 Trim, wash, and shake dry the cabbage, and cut into finger-width strips. Peel the carrots. With the peeler, cut them lengthwise into short strips. Cut the chiles lengthwise, and remove the seeds. Peel and slice the ginger.

3 For the sweet-sour sauce: Trim the onion, finely chop the white part, and thinly slice the green part. Peel and mince the garlic and ginger. In a skillet, heat the oil over medium-low heat. Add the garlic, ginger, and the white onion, and sauté briefly. In a saucepan, mix the stock, ketchup, vinegar, and sugar, and bring to a boil. Reduce the heat and simmer, covered, for 3 minutes. Stir the cornstarch into the water, pour into the pan, and bring to a boil. Cook, stirring, until the sauce thickens. Season with salt and pepper, transfer to serving bowls, and sprinkle with the green part of the onion.

4 Pat the pork dry and cut it into paper-thin slices. Arrange the pork on serving dishes with the carrots and cabbage.

5 Bring the stock to a boil in a fondue pot and place over the heat source. Stir in the chiles, ginger, and soy sauce. To eat, place the pork and vegetables in wire ladles and cook them in the stock. Accompany with the sauce

Dumpling Fondue

● takes a while
● sophisticated

Serves 4:
Dumplings
1 1/2 oz glass noodles
2 sprigs fresh mint
2 sprigs fresh basil
4 oz bean sprouts
1 stalk lemon grass
1/4 cucumber
1 small onion
8 oz pork tenderloin
2 tbs vegetable oil
1 tsp sesame oil
1 tsp finely chopped garlic
1 tsp finely chopped fresh
  ginger
2 tbs soy sauce
1 tbs Thai fish sauce
1/2 tsp five-spice powder
Salt, pepper, & sugar to
  taste
36 sheets rice paper (6
  inch rounds)
1 bunch fresh chives
Hoisin Dipping Sauce:
3/4 cup prepared hoisin
  sauce
6-7 tbs water

3 carrots
1 bunch green onions
1 1/2 cups chicken stock

Prep time: 1 1/2 hours
Per serving approx.: 470 calories
/ 32 g protein / 23 g fat / 37 g
carbohydrates

1 For the dumplings:
Place the glass noodles in
a heatproof bowl and
pour boiling water over
them. Let the noodles
soak for 5 minutes. Drain
the noodles and cut them
into short pieces.

2 Wash and shake dry
the herbs and sprouts.
Chop the herbs. Trim the
lemon grass and finely
chop the lower third of
the stalks. Peel the
cucumber, halve it
lengthwise, remove the
seeds with a spoon, and
dice the cucumber flesh
finely. Peel and mince the
onion. Cut the pork into
short, thin strips.

3 In skillet, heat the oils
over medium-high heat.
Add the pork and sauté
until well browned.
Remove from the heat
and mix in the lemon
grass, cucumber, onion,
garlic, ginger, noodles,
herbs, sprouts, soy sauce,
fish sauce, 5-spice
powder, salt, pepper, and
sugar.

4 Soak 1 piece of rice
paper in a pan of
lukewarm water until
pliable. Transfer to a
towel-lined work surface
and put 1 tsp filling in
the center. Bring the
edges of the rice paper up
to form a bundle and tie
closed with a chive.
Transfer the bundle to a
serving dish and cover
with a damp towel.

Repeat the filling process
with the remaining
ingredients.

5 For the hoisin dipping
sauce: Mix the hoisin
sauce with the water, and
place it in a serving bowl.

6 Trim and wash the
carrots and green onions.
Peel and slice the carrots.
Cut the green onions into
chunks. Arrange the
vegetables on a serving
dish with the dumplings.
Bring the stock to a boil
in a fondue pot and place
it on the table over the
heat source.

7 To eat, place the
dumplings and vegetables
in wire ladles and cook in
the boiling stock.
Accompany with the
sauce.

Smoked Pork Fondue

● takes a while
● easy

Serves 4:
2 onions
1 tbs vegetable oil
2 1/4 cups (18 fl oz) hard cider
2 1/2 cups water
4 juniper berries • 1 bay leaf • 2 whole cloves • 5 black peppercorns
Pumpkin Sauce:
9 oz pumpkin puree (unsweetened)
1 tsp mustard seeds
1/2 cup crème fraîche
Juice from 1/2 orange
Salt, cayenne pepper, & sugar to taste
Cabbage Salad:
1 small head green cabbage
6 tbs cider vinegar
Salt, pepper, & sugar to taste
5 tbs vegetable stock
2/3 cup heavy cream
2 carrots
1 bunch fresh chives
3 oz walnuts, chopped

28 oz boneless smoked pork loin
Mustard sauce, p 20, substituting 1 large shallot for the chives

Prep time: 2 hours
Per serving approx.: 1055 calories / 44 g protein / 74 g fat / 59 g carbohydrates

1 Peel the onions and cut them into strips. In a saucepan, heat the oil over medium heat. Add the onions and sauté until translucent. Add the cider, water, and spices and bring to a boil. Reduce the heat and simmer the mixture for 30 minutes; strain.

2 For the pumpkin sauce: In a saucepan, mix the pumpkin with the mustard seeds, crème fraîche, and orange juice. Heat until just warmed through. Season with salt, cayenne , and sugar.

3 For the cabbage salad: Trim and wash the cabbage, and slice it thinly. Place it in a colander and pour boiling water over it. Push out as much liquid as possible. In a large bowl, mix the vinegar, salt, pepper, sugar, stock, and cream. Add the cabbage and toss well. Cover and let stand for 2 hours. Peel and grate the carrots. Chop the chives finely. Mix in the carrots, chives, and nuts.

4 Cut the pork loin into strips. Bring the onion stock to a boil in the fondue pot, and place it over the heat source. To eat, place the pork in wire ladles and heat in the stock. Accompany with the sauces and salad.

Italian Family-Style Fondue

● can prepare in advance
● takes a while

Serves 4-6:
10 oz oxtails
1 small onion
2 cloves garlic
1 small chicken (about 2-2 1/2 lb)
1 bay leaf
5 peppercorns
2 carrots
1 leek
1/2 bunch fresh Italian parsley
Green Sauce:
4 oz Italian bread
2 bunches fresh Italian parsley
1 bunch fresh chervil
3 cloves garlic
2 hard-boiled eggs
4 oz pickles
1 tbs capers
3 tbs balsamic vinegar
2 tsp anchovy paste
2/3 cup extra-virgin olive oil
Red Pepper Sauce:
1 red bell pepper
1 small onion
2 tbs vegetable oil
1 tsp Hungarian paprika
1 cup heavy cream
Salt, pepper, & sugar to taste

18 oz boneless beef rump
8 oz hard salami

Prep time: 1 1/2 hours
Simmering time: 2 1/2 hours
Per serving (6) approx.: 945 calories / 63 g protein / 62 g fat / 36 g carbohydrates

1 The day before you plan to eat, pour boiling water over the oxtail bones. Transfer the bones to a pot with about 2 quarts of cold water (to cover the bones), and slowly bring to a boil. Reduce the heat to a slow simmer. Peel the onion and garlic and cut them in half.

2 Remove the skin from the chicken and remove the breast meat from the bone. After 1 hour of simmering, add the chicken (except the breast meat), onion, garlic, bay leaf, and peppercorns to the pot, and simmer for another hour. Peel the carrots. Wash the leek and parsley. Roughly chop the carrots, leek, and parsley, and add them to the stock. Simmer the stock for 30 minutes.

3 Strain the stock. Remove the meat from the oxtails and chicken bones, and save for another use. Cool the stock completely overnight. The next day, remove the congealed fat from the surface of the stock, and heat through.

4 For the green sauce: Cut the bread into cubes, put the cubes in a blender, and pour 2/3 cup of the hot stock over it. Wash and shake dry the herbs, and remove the stems. Peel and chop the garlic and eggs. Slice the pickles. Puree the herb leaves and chopped ingredients with the capers, vinegar, and anchovy paste. Add the oil in a thin stream, until creamy.

5 For the red pepper sauce: Trim, wash, and dice the red pepper. Peel and dice the onion. Heat the oil in a skillet over medium heat. Add the onion and pepper and sauté until translucent. Sprinkle with the paprika, and add the cream and 2/3 cup of the stock. Simmer the sauce for 15 minutes, puree finely, and press through a sieve. Season with salt, pepper, and sugar.

6 Cut the chicken breast and beef across the grain into thin slices, and then cut into strips. Peel and slice the salami Place the remaining stock in the fondue pot, bring to a boil, and place over the heat source. To eat, put the chicken, beef, and salami in a wire ladle and cook in the hot stock. Accompany with the sauces.

above: Italian Family-Style Fondue
below: Smoked Pork Fondue

Venison Fondue

● sophisticated
● low-cal

Serves 4:
1 1/2 lb boneless venison meat (haunch or saddle)
1 3/4 lb vegetables (such as Brussels sprouts, cauliflower, carrots)
Salt to taste
3 1/3 cups light meat stock
1 cup dry white wine (or water)
1 sprig fresh thyme
2 juniper berries, crushed
1 bay leaf
Pepper to taste
Purchased steak sauce

Prep time: 50 minutes
Freezing time: 1 hour
Per serving approx.: 450 calories / 43 g protein / 12 g fat / 21 g carbohydrates

1 Wrap the venison in plastic wrap and freeze for about 1 hour.

2 Meanwhile, trim and wash all vegetables. Leave Brussels sprouts whole. Break cauliflower into florets. Peel carrots and cut them into chunks. Separate the vegetables by type and cook each separately in boiling, salted water for about 5 minutes. Plunge the vegetables into cold water to stop the cooking and drain. Arrange the vegetables on dishes.

3 Pour the meat stock, white wine, thyme, juniper berries, and bay leaf into the fondue pot and bring to a boil.

4 Slice the venison thinly across the grain using a sharp knife. Arrange the meat on a serving dish and sprinkle the slices lightly with pepper.

5 Place the fondue pot on the table over the heat source. To eat, pierce the meat and vegetables with fondue forks and cook them in the stock. Accompany with the steak sauce.

Serving suggestions: serve with bread, Potato Garlic Sauce (p 58) and Zucchini Relish (p 54).

Wine Fondue

● easy
● sophisticated

Serves 4:
14 oz boneless veal or beef tenderloin
14 oz boneless lamb
2 carrots
1 leek
1/2 bunch fresh Italian parsley
3 1/3 cups light meat stock
1 bay leaf
1 tsp peppercorns
1 tsp allspice berries
Salsa Verde:
4 bunches fresh Italian parsley
3 anchovy fillets
1 clove garlic
2 tbs capers
10 tbs olive oil
2 tsp balsamic vinegar
2 tsp fresh lemon juice
Salt & pepper to taste

2 1/2 cups dry white wine

Prep time: 30 minutes
Time in freezer: 1 hour
Per serving approx.: 890 calories / 42 g protein / 58 g fat / 34 g carbohydrates

1 Wrap the meats separately in plastic wrap and freeze them for about 1 hour.

2 Meanwhile, peel or trim, wash, and chop the carrots, leek, and parsley, and add them to a saucepan with the meat stock, bay leaf, crushed peppercorns, and allspice. Bring the stock to a boil, then reduce the heat to low. Simmer, covered, for about 15 minutes.

3 For the salsa verde: Wash and shake dry the parsley, and pick off the leaves. Rinse the anchovy fillets. Peel the garlic. In a blender, puree the above ingredients together with the capers. Add the oil in a thin stream to produce a thick sauce. Stir in the balsamic vinegar and lemon juice, and season with salt and pepper.

4 Pat the meats dry. Slice the meats thinly across the grain and arrange on a serving dish. Pour the stock through a colander into a fondue pot. Add the wine, bring to a boil, and place on the table over the heat source.

5 To eat, roll up the meat slices and spear them with fondue forks. Cook the meat rolls in the hot broth and accompany with the salsa verde.

above: Venison Fondue
below: Wine Fondue

Vegetable Fondue with Three Sauces

● easy
● can prepare in advance

Serves 4:
Tuna Sauce:
1 can water-packed tuna
   (6 oz), drained
1/3 cup crème fraîche
3 tbs fresh lemon juice
2 tbs chopped fresh chives
Salt & pepper to taste
Curried Cheese Sauce:
5 oz feta cheese, crumbled
1/2 cup milk
1 tsp mild curry powder
2 tbs chopped fresh Italian
   parsley
Pepper to taste
1 tomato
Basil Sauce:
2 shallots
2 bunches fresh basil
1 tsp mustard
3 tbs red wine vinegar
2 tbs balsamic vinegar
1/2 cup extra-virgin olive
   oil
Salt & pepper to taste

3 1/2–4 lb spring
   vegetables (such as baby
   carrots, asparagus, sugar-
   snap peas)
1 1/2 quarts vegetable
   stock

Prep time: 1 hour
Per serving approx.: 785 calories
/ 37 g protein / 37 g fat / 82 g
carbohydrates

1 For the tuna sauce:
Place the tuna in a
blender and puree it finely
with the crème fraîche
and lemon juice. Fold in
the chives and season
with salt and pepper.

2 For the cheese sauce:
Put the cheese in a
saucepan with the milk
and curry. Stir over low
heat until melted. Puree
the mixture with the
parsley, using a hand
blender or regular
blender, and season with
pepper. Wash the tomato,
dice it finely, and fold
into the sauce.

3 For the basil sauce:
Peel and finely mince the
shallots. Wash and shake
dry the basil, and chop
the leaves. Place both
ingredients in a bowl and
mix with the mustard,
vinegars, oil, salt, and
pepper.

4 Trim and wash all of
the vegetables, peel if
necessary, and cut into
bite-sized pieces. Arrange
the vegetables on serving
dishes. Pour the sauces
into small bowls.

5 Bring the stock to a
boil in the fondue pot,
and place it on the table
over the heat source. To
eat, place the vegetables
in wire ladles and cook in
the hot stock until
tender-crisp. Accompany
with the sauces.

Viennese Fondue

● sophisticated
○ takes a while

Serves 4:
8 oz beef liver
1 lb beef fillet
Vegetable-Bean Salad:
2 leeks
3 carrots
7 oz celery root
1 small onion
1 can white beans (15 oz)
1 bay leaf
Salt to taste
Small handful celery leaves
5 tbs white wine vinegar
Pepper & sugar to taste
5 tbs sunflower oil
2 tbs pumpkin seed oil
Apple-Horseradish Sauce:
2 stale white rolls
1/2 cup light meat stock
4 tart apples
1 tbs cider vinegar
1 tbs sunflower oil
1 tsp sugar
1 piece fresh horseradish
   root (1 inch)

4 cups meat stock
1 cup dry white wine (or
   stock)
Chive Vinaigrette, p 21,
   without the tomato

Prep. time: 1 1/2 hours
Marinating time: 3 hours
Per serving approx.: 970 calories
/ 45 g protein / 50 g fat / 69 g
carbohydrates

1 Skin and clean the
liver. Pat dry the liver and
fillet. Cut each into thin
slices, and then into
strips. Arrange the meats
on a serving dish.

2 For the salad: Trim the
leeks, halve them
lengthwise, wash them
well, and cut into 1/4-
inch strips. Peel the
carrots and celery root,
and cut each into 1/3-
inch cubes. Peel and dice
the onion. Rinse the
beans in a colander.

3 Place the carrots,
celery root, onion, and
bay leaf in boiling salted
water for 10 minutes. For
the last 3 minutes, add
the leeks. Drain the
vegetables, setting aside
5 tbs of the cooking
water. Plunge the
vegetables into ice water
to stop the cooking.

4 Wash, shake dry, and
chop the celery leaves,
and add to a large bowl.
Add the vinegar, salt,
pepper, sugar, vegetable
cooking water, and oils
and whisk well. Add the
drained vegetables, toss
well, cover the bowl, and
marinate for 2 hours.

5 For the apple-
horseradish sauce:
Remove the crusts from
the rolls, cut the rolls into
thin slices, place them in
a bowl, and pour over the
stock. Peel and core the

apples, dice them coarsely, and mix with the vinegar. Heat the oil in a skillet over medium heat. Add the apples and sugar, sauté briefly, then simmer, covered, for 3–5 minutes; the apples should still be crunchy. Peel the horseradish and grate it coarsely. Mash the apple mixture coarsely, then mix in the soaked rolls and the grated horseradish.

7 Bring the stock and white wine to a boil in the fondue pot, and place on the table over the heat source. To eat, spear the meats on fondue forks and cook them in the stock. Accompany with the salad and dipping sauces, and vinaigrette.

above: Vegetable Fondue
below: Viennese Fondue

Fondue was already present in ancient China. It was invented by the Mongolians, who, on cold winter evenings, would gather around a charcoal-fueled "hot pot" filled with bubbling stock, chopped vegetables, and lamb, warming themselves both inside and out.

The Hot Pot

Also called a fire pot, the original hot pot got its name because it used to stand over an open fire. The smoke created by the fire was drawn out through the pot's "chimney." Although the hot pot has retained the same basic shape—with its wide cooking channel and chimney in the middle—it is now usually heated over a burner, external heat source (such as sterno), or by an electrical wall outlet. Hot pots are available in aluminum, brass, copper, or stainless steel. Their 2- to 2 1/2-quart capacity is greater than that of a standard fondue pot. If you eat fondue often, it's worth investing in a hot pot. However, any of the hot pot recipes in this book can be prepared just as easily using a standard meat fondue set.

Basic equipment for Asian fondue: hot pot, wire ladles, bowls, chopsticks, and ceramic spoons

International Fondues

Eating Authentically

If you enjoy decorating your table along an Asian theme, set it with small bowls, wire ladles, and chopsticks, as well as ceramic spoons for the soup at the end of the meal. The hot pot or fondue pot serves as the centerpiece. Around it you can place the beautifully arranged serving dishes lined with the finely chopped ingredients, dipping sauces, and side dishes. Be sure to serve a large bowl of rice.

During the meal, the hot pot is filled—at least halfway—with hot stock. The extra stock is kept warm for filling the pot throughout the meal as needed. Each person dips his or her own ingredients into the hot broth.

Depending on the size of the pieces, meat and fish are often cooked within several seconds. Vegetables should be cooked only until they achieve a pleasant crunchiness. Everything is then retrieved from the pot with the wire ladle or chopsticks, placed in the small bowls, and mixed with rice and dipping sauces as desired.

At the end of the meal, the savory broth is ladled into soup bowls and enjoyed as the meal's finale.

Far-Eastern Ingredients

One of the reasons Asian cuisine is so good for you is because it uses only the freshest ingredients. Most of the exotic vegetables, herbs, and spices can be purchased in Asian markets, or in high-quality supermarkets. Look for fresh ginger, chiles, cilantro, and shiitake mushrooms. Good-quality bamboo shoots are available in small cans.

Eating with Chopsticks

For some reason, Asian fondue tastes even better when eaten with chopsticks. Using chopsticks really isn't hard to do once you get the hang of it. Here's how: Clamp the bottom chopstick in the bend of your thumb and support it on the tip of your partially extended ring finger.

Hold the top chopstick like a pencil between the tips of your thumb, index finger, and middle finger. When you pick something up, the bottom chopstick remains stationary while the top chopstick moves up and down. Practice picking up different objects with your chopsticks to prepare for your next Asian meal.

Asian ingredients from left to right: fresh ginger, bean sprouts, fresh cilantro, red chiles, shiitake mushrooms, lemon grass

Chinese Hot Pot

● sophisticated
● takes a while

Serves 6–8:
1 lb pork tenderloin
1 lb boneless chicken
  breasts
Ginger Sauce:
1 piece fresh ginger (about
  1 inch)
1 clove garlic
1 green onion
1 fresh red chile
1/4 cup light soy sauce
2 tbs sake (rice wine) or
  dry sherry
1 tsp sesame oil
Sweet–Sour Sauce (page
  32)
2 oz glass noodles
8 oz cauliflower
8 oz carrots
6 oz Savoy cabbage
6 oz cucumbers
6 oz bean sprouts
1 can bamboo shoots
  (8 oz)
1 can water chestnuts
  (8 oz)
8 oz sole or flounder fillets
8 oz shrimp
2 1/2 quarts light chicken
  stock
2 tbs chopped fresh
  cilantro or chives
Soy sauce to taste

Prep time: 1 1/2 hours
Freezing time: 1 hour
Per serving (8) approx.: 440
calories / 54 g protein / 15 g fat
/ 21 g carbohydrates

1 Wrap the pork and chicken separately in plastic wrap and freeze for about 1 hour.

2 For the ginger sauce: Peel the ginger and garlic. Trim the green onion and red chile. Finely chop all ingredients and place in a bowl. Add the soy sauce, sake, and sesame oil and mix well.

3 Put the ginger sauce and sweet-sour sauce in small serving bowls.

4 Put the glass noodles in a heatproof bowl, pour boiling water over them, and let them soak for 5 minutes. Drain the noodles thoroughly. Using scissors, cut the noodles into short pieces; cover, and set aside.

5 Trim, peel if necessary, and wash the fresh vegetables. Separate the cauliflower into small florets. Cut the carrots into matchstick strips. Cut the cabbage leaves into 1-inch-wide strips. Halve the cucumber lengthwise, then cut it into 1/4-inch slices. Wash the bean sprouts and drain thoroughly.

6 Drain the bamboo shoots and water chestnuts separately. Cut the bamboo shoots into 1/4-inch slices.

7 Remove the pork and chicken from the freezer and remove the plastic wrap. With a sharp knife, cut the pork and chicken into paper-thin slices, cutting across the grain. Cut the fish fillets into very thin slices.

8 Remove the shells from the shrimp. Devein the shrimp: With a small sharp knife, carefully split the shrimp lengthwise along their backs and remove the dark vein inside. Rinse the shrimp and pat dry thoroughly.

9 Arrange all the prepared ingredients on serving dishes and place on the table.

10 In a saucepan, bring the chicken stock to a boil. Transfer the stock to a hot pot (you can also use a meat fondue pot, small wok, or a pretty saucepan) and place it on the table over the heat source. Keep the stock simmering slightly throughout the meal.

11 To eat, place any combination of ingredients (except the glass noodles) in wire ladles and cook them in the stock.

12 Using chopsticks, dip the cooked ingredients in the sauces and eat.

13 When finished with the fondue, heat the glass noodles in the remaining stock and sprinkle with the cilantro. Season the broth with soy sauce and serve hot in Asian bowls or soup cups.

Variations

You can use any type of tender, lean meat for this dish, such as beef tenderloin or boneless turkey breast. Mushrooms are a also good meaty substitute. Suitable vegetables include leeks, sugar snap peas, broccoli, green onions, and bell peppers. If you're in a hurry, you can use purchased dipping sauces instead of making your own.

Mongolian Hot Pot

● can prepare in advance
● sophisticated

Serves 6:
2 1/2 lb boneless leg of lamb
1/2 oz dried shiitake mushrooms
8 oz thin Asian egg noodles
10 oz Savoy cabbage
10 oz celery
10 oz fresh spinach
1 bunch fresh cilantro
1 tbs sesame oil
Soy sauce, prepared plum sauce, prepared hoisin sauce
2 1/2 quarts chicken stock

Prep time: 40 minutes
Freezing time: 1 hour
Per serving approx.: 820 calories / 52 g protein / 39 g fat / 66 g carbohydrates

1 Wrap the lamb in plastic wrap and freeze for about 1 hour.

2 Place the mushrooms in a heatproof bowl, pour boiling water over them, and soak for 30 minutes. Cook the noodles according to the directions on the package.

3 Trim and wash the cabbage, celery, and spinach. Cut the cabbage into finger-width strips. Slice the celery diagonally. Cut the large spinach leaves in half.

Wash and shake dry the cilantro, then remove the leaves from the stems. Strain the mushrooms, rinse them, and pat them dry thoroughly. Arrange all above ingredients on serving dishes.

4 Cut the lamb across the grain into paper-thin slices. Arrange the slices on a serving dish and brush with the sesame oil. Pour the sauces into bowls for dipping.

5 In a saucepan, bring the chicken stock to a boil. Transfer the stock to a hot pot.

6 To eat, place the vegetables, mushrooms, noodles, and meat in wire ladles and cook them in the stock. Using chopsticks, dip the cooked ingredients into the dipping sauces and eat. Accompany the cooked ingredients with the cilantro. When finished, season the broth with soy sauce and serve in small soup bowls.

Korean Hot Pot

● easy
● sophisticated

Serves 6:
1/2 oz dried Asian mushrooms
8 oz beef fillet
8 oz boneless chicken breasts
1 clove garlic
1 tsp sugar
3 tbs light soy sauce
2 tbs sake (rice wine) or dry sherry
8 oz lean ground pork or beef
1 egg yolk
Salt & pepper to taste
4 drops sesame oil
1 tbs finely chopped fresh cilantro
8 oz carrots
8 oz green onions
8 oz broccoli
6 oz small shrimp, peeled
8 oz mild white fish fillet
8 oz firm marinated tofu
Soy Dipping Sauce:
2/3 cup light soy sauce
1/4 cup rice vinegar
2 tbs sesame seeds, toasted
1/2 green onion, very finely chopped

2 1/2 quarts light beef stock
2 green onions, finely chopped
1 fresh red chile, finely chopped

Prep time: 50 minutes
Per serving approx.: 470 calories / 40 g protein / 20 g fat / 37 g carbohydrates

1 Place the mushrooms in a heatproof bowl, pour boiling water over them,

and let them soak for 30 minutes. Meanwhile, cut the beef across the grain into paper-thin slices. Cut the chicken breast into cubes. Arrange both on serving dishes.

2 Peel and mince the garlic. Mix the garlic with the sugar, 2 tbs of the soy sauce, and the sake. Brush the mixture on the beef and chicken, cover the dishes, and refrigerate until serving time.

3 Mix the ground meat with the egg yolk, salt, pepper, oil, remaining 1 tbs soy sauce, and the cilantro. Wet your hands and form walnut-sized meatballs from this mixture. Arrange the meatballs on a serving dish, cover, and chill until serving time.

4 Trim, peel if necessary, and wash the carrots, green onions, and broccoli. Cut each into small, decorative pieces. Pat dry the shrimp and fish fillet. Peel and devein the shrimp (see p 42, step 8). Cut the fillet into thin slices. Strain the soaked mushrooms, rinse, and pat dry thoroughly. Cut

the tofu into small cubes.

5 For the soy dipping sauce: mix all the ingredients together and pour into 6 small bowls.

6 Arrange the fish, shrimp, vegetables, mushrooms, and tofu on serving dishes, and place them on the table with the beef, chicken, and meatballs. In a saucepan, bring the stock to a boil. Transfer the stock to a hot pot.

7 To eat, place any combination of ingredients in wire ladles and cook in the stock. Using chopsticks, dip the cooked ingredients in the soy dipping sauce. When everything has been eaten, finish the broth by adding the chopped green onions and chile to the stock, and eat the soup in small bowls.

above: Mongolian Hot Pot
below: Korean Hot Pot

Sukiyaki

● sophisticated
● can prepare in advance

Serves 4:

4 oz glass noodles
8 oz firm tofu
1 bunch green onions
6 oz baby Swiss chard (or spinach)
8 fresh shiitake mushrooms (or large white mushrooms)
18 oz boneless beef rump
1/4 cup sake (dry rice wine) or dry sherry
1/4 cup mirin (sweet rice wine) or cream sherry
1/2 cup chicken stock
1/2 cup soy sauce
1 tbs sugar
4 fresh egg yolks (unbroken)
2 tbs canola oil
Pepper to taste

Prep time: 50 minutes
Per serving approx.: 640 calories / 35 g protein / 37 g fat / 35 g carbohydrates

1 Place the noodles in a heatproof bowl, pour boiling water over them, and soak for 5 minutes. Strain the noodles and cut them into small pieces with scissors. Cut the tofu into cubes.

2 Trim and wash the onions, chard, and shiitakes. Cut the onions into pieces. Remove the hard stems from chard and quarter the leaves. Remove the stems from the mushrooms.

3 Cut the meat into thin slices, then cut it into narrow strips.

4 In a small saucepan, mix together the sake, mirin, stock, soy sauce, and sugar, and heat until steaming. Transfer the mixture to a pitcher. Arrange the noodles, tofu, vegetables, and beef on serving dishes. Place 1 egg yolk in each of 4 small bowls and place a bowl in front of each placesetting.

5 To eat, heat the oil in a small wok or wide saucepan and place it on the table over the heat source. Brown a small amount of the meat in the oil until it is half-cooked, and push it to the side of the pan. Add 1/3 of the remaining ingredients and 1/2 of the stock mixture. Simmer the ingredients briefly.

6 With chopsticks, dip the cooked ingredients in the egg yolk. Gradually cook the remaining ingredients. The bottom of the pot should just barely be covered with stock, the ingredients should simmer rather than boil. If the stock boils down too much, add water.

Shabu Shabu

● sophisticated
● low-cal

Serves 6:

Sesame Sauce:
6 tbs sesame seeds
1 tbs sugar
1 tbs miso (fermented soybean paste)
3 tbs mirin (sweet rice wine) or cream sherry
3 tbs rice vinegar
2 tbs sake (dry rice wine) or dry sherry
6 tbs soy sauce
1 tsp dry mustard
Ponzu Sauce:
1/2 cup fresh lemon juice
1/4 cup soy sauce
3 tbs water

1 piece daikon radish (6 oz)
2 green onions
3 carrots
2 small leeks
8 oz Chinese cabbage
18 small shiitake mushrooms
8 oz firm tofu
20 oz beef fillet
6 cups light chicken stock
1 piece kombu (dried seaweed—optional)

Prep time: 1 1/4 hours
Per serving approx.: 450 calories / 27 g protein / 25 g fat / 30 g carbohydrates

1 For the sesame sauce: Lightly brown the sesame seeds in a dry nonstick skillet. Transfer them to a blender and whirl briefly. Add the remaining sauce ingredients and blend briefly. Pour the sauce into 6 small bowls.

2 For the ponzu sauce: Stir the lemon juice, soy sauce, and water together, and pour into 6 small serving bowls.

3 Peel and grate the radish (not too finely). Trim the green onions and cut them into paper-thin slices. Place each in a separate bowl.

4 Trim, peel, and slice the carrots. Trim, wash, and slice the leeks. Wash the cabbage and cut it into 1-inch strips. Wipe clean the mushrooms and break off the stems.

5 Cut the tofu into cubes. Cut the meat across the grain into paper-thin slices, and arrange on a serving dish. In a saucepan, combine the chicken stock and kombu (if using) and bring to a boil.

6 Arrange the vegetables, mushrooms, and tofu on a serving dish. Remove the kombu from the stock. Transfer the stock to a hot pot. Place the bowls of sesame sauce, ponzu sauce, green onions, and radish on the table.

7 To eat, place the vegetables, mushrooms and tofu in wire ladles and cook in the stock. Using chopsticks, dip the meat slices individually into the lightly simmering stock, moving them back and forth once, just so that they lose their red color. Then, dip the cooked meat in one of the sauces. Each person seasons his or her own sauces at the table—the sesame sauce with green onions and the ponzu sauce with the radish and/or green onions.

Tip! The egg yolk—a traditional Japanese ingredient—serves as a natural, creamy dipping sauce. Though the hot food cooks the egg yolk on contact, you may wish to substitute 2 tbs pasteurized frozen egg yolks for each fresh yolk, if you are concerned about the safety of the eggs in your area

above: **Shabu Shabu**
below: **Sukiyaki**

Bagna Cauda

(Piedmontese Vegetable Fondue)

● easy
● inexpensive

Serves 4:
14 oz broccoli
1 bulb fennel
2 small heads radicchio
4 stalks celery
1 yellow bell pepper
1 red bell pepper
1 green bell pepper
2 zucchini
Salt to taste
2 small baguettes
Anchovy Sauce:
4 oz anchovy fillets
3-5 cloves garlic
1/4 cup butter
1 cup olive oil

Prep time: 1 hour
Per serving approx.: 1240
calories / 32 g protein / 66 g fat
/ 138 g carbohydrates

1 Trim and wash the broccoli, fennel, radicchio, celery, bell peppers, and zucchini. Separate the broccoli into small florets. Plunge the florets into boiling salted water for 5 minutes. Remove the florets and plunge them into ice water; drain. Cut the fennel into eighths. Cut the radicchio into quarters. Cut the celery into bite-sized pieces, and cut all of the bell peppers into strips. Quarter the zucchini lengthwise, and cut the zucchini into 1 1/2-inch pieces.

2 Cut the baguettes into finger-width slices. Arrange the bread and vegetable pieces on serving dishes.

3 For the anchovy sauce: Rinse the anchovies under cold running water, pat dry, and chop. Peel and finely chop the garlic.

4 In a skillet, melt the butter over low heat. Add the garlic and sauté briefly; take care that it doesn't brown. Add the olive oil and heat, making sure that the garlic stays light-colored. Remove the pan from the stove.

5 With a fork, finely mash the anchovies and add them to the pan. Place the skillet over low heat and stir until a creamy sauce forms.

6 Place the pan on a stand on the table, over the heat source. To eat, dunk the vegetables in the hot (but not boiling) anchovy sauce. Accompany with the bread.

American-Style Fondue

● can prepare in advance
● easy

Serves 4:
Orange Sauce:
2 oranges
8 oz cream cheese,
  softened
2 tbs chopped fresh chives
Salt & white pepper to
  taste
Creamy Tomato Sauce:
2/3 cup light mayonnaise
2/3 cup ketchup
2 tbs tomato paste
1 tbs brandy (optional)
Pinch of sugar
Salt & cayenne pepper to
  taste
1 tbs small diced tomato

18 oz boneless turkey
  breast
10 oz beef fillet
2 fresh ears corn
6 cups vegetable oil
Salt & pepper to taste

Prep time: 30 minutes
Per serving approx.: 850 calories
/ 45 g protein / 55 g fat / 49 g
carbohydrates

1 For the orange sauce:
Peel 1 of the oranges,
divide it into sections,
and cut the sections into
small pieces.

2 Rinse the remaining
orange in hot water, pat
dry, and remove thin
strips of the zest with a
zester; set aside. Squeeze
the orange juice and stir
it into the cream cheese
until smooth. Fold in the
orange pieces and chives.
Season the sauce with
salt and pepper, place in a
serving bowl, and garnish
with the orange zest.

3 For the creamy tomato
sauce: stir together the
mayonnaise, ketchup,
tomato paste, brandy (if
using), and sugar until
smooth. Season with salt
and cayenne pepper.
Place the sauce in a
serving bowl and garnish
with the diced tomato.

4 Pat dry the turkey and
beef, and cut them into
bite-sized cubes. Shuck
the corn, removing all of
the silk. With a large,
sharp knife, carefully cut
the corn cobs into 1-inch
pieces. Arrange the
turkey, beef, and corn
pieces on serving dishes.

5 Heat the oil in a
fondue pot to 350°F and
place it on the table over
the heat source. To eat,
pierce the turkey and
meat cubes and corn cobs
with fondue forks and
cook them in the hot oil.
Season each piece with
salt and pepper as
desired, and accompany
with the dipping sauces.

Swiss Cheese Fondue

● fast
● vegetarian

Serves 4:
1 loaf crusty white bread
  (24 oz)
10 oz Gruyère cheese
10 oz Swiss Emmenthaler
  cheese
1 clove garlic
1 1/4 cups dry white wine
2 tsp fresh lemon juice
2 tsp cornstarch
1/4 cup kirschwasser
  (cherry brandy)
Freshly grated nutmeg to
  taste
White pepper to taste

Prep time: 30 minutes
Per serving approx.: 1185
calories / 59 g protein / 51 g fat
/ 97 g carbohydrates

1 Cut the bread into
finger-width slices, then
cut it into bite-sized
chunks. Arrange the bread
in a basket or on a
serving dish.

2 Remove the rinds from
the cheeses and dice
them. Peel the garlic,
halve it lengthwise, and
rub it vigorously around
the inside of a cheese
fondue pot.

3 Pour the white wine
and lemon juice into the
fondue pot and bring to a
boil over medium heat.
Gradually add the diced
cheeses to the pot, and
cook over low heat,
stirring constantly in a
figure-eight pattern, until
the mixture is smooth
and creamy.

4 Stir the cornstarch into
the kirschwasser until
smooth, pour it into the
cheese mixture, and bring
it to a boil, stirring
constantly. Remove the
pot from the stove, and
season the cheese
mixture with nutmeg and
pepper. Place the fondue
pot on the table over the
heat source.

5 To eat, spear the bread
chunks with fondue forks
and dip them into the
cheese mixture.

Tip! Instead of white
bread, this also tastes
great with a dense rye
bread. For an extra
indulgence (adults only!),
you can soak a cube of
either type of bread in
kirsch before dunking it
into the cheese sauce.

Fonduta

(Piedmontese cheese
fondue)

● vegetarian
● sophisticated

Serves 4:
18 oz Italian Fontina
  cheese
1 cup milk
1 crusty baguette
10 oz broccoli
2 carrots
Salt to taste
1 tbs butter
2 tsp flour
3 egg yolks
White pepper to taste

Prep time: 45 minutes
Soaking time: 3-4 hours
Per serving approx.: 940 calories
/ 48 g protein / 51 g fat / 72 g
carbohydrates

1 Remove the rind from
the cheese and dice it.
Place the cheese in a
bowl, pour over the milk,
cover, and let the cheese
soak for at least 3-4
hours, or overnight.

2 Cut the baguette into
bite-sized chunks. Trim
and wash the broccoli,
and separate it into small
florets. Peel the thick
broccoli stalks and cut
them into 1/4-inch slices.
Peel the carrots, rinse,
and cut them diagonally
into 1/4-inch slices.

3 Plunge the broccoli
florets, broccoli stalks,
and carrots in boiling
salted water for 5
minutes. Drain the
vegetables, plunging
them immediately into
ice water, and drain
thoroughly. Arrange the
bread, broccoli, and
carrots on serving dishes.

4 In a small saucepan,
melt the butter over
medium heat. Add the
flour and stir until the
mixture is slightly
browned. Transfer the
mixture to a stainless
steel bowl.

5 Place the bowl over a
pan of simmering water,
taking care that the
bottom of the bowl does
not touch the water. Add
the cheese and milk to
the bowl. Melt the cheese
over low heat while
stirring vigorously; the
mixture will be slightly
stringy. Caution: The
water must only simmer
slightly, not boil.

6 As soon as the cheese
is completely melted,
increase the heat. Add
the egg yolks one at a
time while stirring
vigorously. Continue
stirring in a figure-eight
pattern until you have a
thick, creamy mixture
that is no longer stringy.

7 Season the cheese mixture with pepper, transfer to a preheated cheese fondue pot, and place on the table over the heat source. The mixture should remain hot, but it must not boil or it will become runny.

8 To eat, spear the bread chunks, broccoli, or carrot pieces with a fondue fork and dip them into the cheese mixture.

Tip! If you feel like splurging, enjoy your Fonduta with paper-thin slices of fresh white truffle, in authentic Piedmont style. If you can't find Fontina, you can substitute young provolone or another soft-textured cow's milk cheese.

above: Fonduta
below: Swiss Cheese Fondue

Salads, chutneys, pickles, relishes, and herb sauces round out the culinary spectrum of a hearty fondue. Salads should be as fresh as possible when served. Chutneys, pickles, relishes and herb sauces, such as pesto, are excellent when prepared a couple of days in advance. If you preserve them in screw-top jars, you can even keep them for several weeks or even months. These zesty side dishes are good with all kinds of savory fondues.

Sauces and Side Dishes

The sauces and side dishes are what make your fondue a success. Start with the the fondues, sauces and side dishes you find inside. Then, combine fondue ingredients from one recipe with the sauces from another recipe to come up with your own unique creations. If you're in a hurry, you can find a large selection of prepared sauces in supermarkets and specialty food stores. In addition to the recipes in this book, you can serve fondue with any type of green salad or vegetable salad, and with prepared chutneys and relishes. Though the Asian fondues should be accompanied by rice, serve other types of fondue with an abundance of bread.

Side Dishes and Sweet Fondues

Be sure to carefully follow your recipe for preserving homemade chutneys and relishes. Most recipes recommend turning the jars upside-down after filling to help keep both oxygen and bacteria from getting into the food, leading to spoilage.

What to Do with Leftovers

Cover vegetables, salads, and sauces and place them in the refrigerator. They'll taste good the next day with boiled potatoes and meat, hamburgers, or cold cuts. Uneaten meat, poultry, and fish should be cooked, then cooled, wrapped, and refrigerated. Leftover rice can be mixed with a few vegetables, an onion, and a little curry paste to make a tasty rice bowl for tomorrow's lunch. Leftover vegetables can be used to make soup.

Something Sweet

Children aren't the only fans of sweet fondues. Adults are also very fond of them, especially as dessert after a light meal or as part of a fondue party. You don't need any fancy equipment to prepare sweet fondues. A pretty, small saucepan is perfect. To keep the fondue warm, use a small electric hot plate, or special sweet fondue warmer with one or two tea-light candles. Fondue forks work best for spearing ingredients.

Variety is the Spice of Life

As with savory fondues, you can improvise sweet fondues to your heart's content. In addition to the traditional chocolate, there are also lighter prepared fondue bases on the market, such as vanilla, and various types of domestic and exotic fruit. You can refine your fondues by stirring in spices, walnuts, almonds, or raisins. If no children are eating, you can also use various liqueurs, fruit brandies, sherries, or cognac.

A Special Treat— Sherry Sabayon

Though not exactly fondue, this sophisticated, light, airy sauce is perfect for dipping fresh fruit or pound cake. In a stainless steel bowl, combine 3 egg yolks and 1 whole egg with 1/4 cup of sugar and beat until creamy, but not foamy. Place the bowl over a pan of simmering water, taking

Various cookies and fresh fruit are the ideal accompaniment to warm Sherry Sabayon

care that the bottom of the bowl doesn't touch the water. Add 10 tbs of sherry—any type works fine. Beat all the ingredients until thick and creamy, taking care that the mixture does not boil. Immediately pour the sabayon into a preheated heatproof bowl and place on a warmer. To eat, pierce pieces of fresh fruit or cake with fondue forks and dip them in the warm sabayon. Serves 4-6 adults.

About Dippers

Almost anything that is firm and has a sweet or sweet-sour taste is a

into sweet fondues. Fruit should be washed, peeled (if necessary), and dried. Berries, dates, cherries, kumquats, and grapes can be left whole, pitted if necessary. Other types of fruit should be cut into bite-sized chunks. Fruit that discolors quickly when exposed to air, such as apples, pears, bananas and apricots, can be drizzled with lemon juice immediately after cutting to prevent discoloration. Sweet fondues taste good accompanied by cookies, ladyfingers, meringues, and firm cake cubes.

Sweet & Spicy Vegetables

● easy
● low-cal

Serves 4:
8 oz broccoli or
  cauliflower
1 carrot
1 small yellow bell pepper
4 oz cherry tomatoes
2 miniature corncobs
  (from a jar)
1 piece fresh ginger (1
  inch)
2 small fresh red chiles
3 tbs vegetable oil
1 bay leaf
2 whole cloves
2 tbs mild curry powder
1/2 tsp ground coriander
Salt to taste
3 tbs sugar
2/3 cup white wine
  vinegar
1 tsp grated lemon zest
1 1/4 cups water

Prep time: 40 minutes
Marinating time: 1–2 days
Per serving approx.: 190 calories
/ 3 g protein / 6 g fat / 33 g
carbohydrates

1 Trim and wash the
broccoli or cauliflower,
carrot, bell pepper, and
tomatoes. Separate the
broccoli or cauliflower
into small florets. Peel the
carrot and cut it
diagonally into thin slices.
Cut the bell pepper into
small strips. Cut the
tomatoes in half.

2 Drain the corn. Peel
and mince the ginger.
Trim the chiles, halve

them lengthwise, remove
the seeds, and cut them
into thin strips.

3 In a saucepan, heat the
oil over medium heat.
Add the bay leaf and
cloves and sauté until
they are aromatic.
Remove the pan from the
heat. Add the curry
powder and coriander and
sauté briefly. Add the salt,
sugar, vinegar, lemon zest,
and water and mix well.

4 Bring the mixture to a
boil. Add all of the
vegetables, except the
corn and tomatoes. Boil
the vegetables for about
4 minutes.

5 Remove the pan from
the heat. Stir in the corn
and tomatoes, then
return the pot to the
heat, and boil all
ingredients for 1 more
minute. Cover the pot and
let the vegetables cool in
the cooking liquid.
Refrigerate the covered
vegetables for at least 1
day, preferably 2 days,
stirring frequently.

6 To serve, drain the
vegetable mixture
thoroughly and put in a
serving bowl.

Zucchini Relish

● can prepare in advance
● inexpensive

Serves 4:
18 oz zucchini
5 shallots
1 tart apple
1/4 cup sugar
1/2 tsp salt
1/4 cup dry sherry
1 bay leaf
1 tsp multicolored
  peppercorns
2 cloves garlic
2/3 cup herb or white wine
  vinegar
2 tsp prepared horseradish
2 tbs olive oil
2 tbs chopped fresh Italian
  parsley

Prep time: 40 minutes
Marinating time: Overnight
Per serving approx.: 230 calories
/ 3 g protein / 7 g fat / 38 g
carbohydrates

1 The evening before
serving, trim and wash
the zucchini. Peel the
shallots. Finely dice the
zucchini and shallots. Peel
the apple, quarter it,
remove the core, and dice
it small.

2 In a bowl, mix the
diced zucchini, shallots,
and apple with the sugar,
salt, and sherry. Cover
and marinate overnight in
a cool place.

3 The next day, pour the
mixture into a colander,
collecting the liquid in a

wide saucepan. Add the
bay leaf and slightly
crushed peppercorns. Peel
and mince the garlic, and
add it to the pan. Boil the
mixture uncovered over
high heat until it is
reduced by half.

4 Add the vinegar and
the fruit and vegetable
pieces to the pan.
Simmer, uncovered, over
medium heat until most
of the liquid has
evaporated, stirring
occasionally. Remove the
bay leaf.

5 Stir in the horseradish
and let the mixture cool.
Just before serving, stir in
the oil and parsley.

above: Sweet & Spicy
Vegetables
below: Zucchini Relish

Tomato-Chutney

 inexpensive
● low-cal

Serves 4:
1 tbs yellow mustard seeds
2 tbs white wine vinegar, plus more to taste
5 tbs water
8 oz cornichons (pickled gherkins)
1 onion
18 oz tomatoes
1 tsp sugar
Salt & pepper to taste
1 tbs tomato paste
3 tbs dry sherry

Prep time: 40 minutes
Per serving approx.: 70 calories / 2 g protein / 1 g fat / 11 g carbohydrates

1 In a saucepan, place the mustard seeds, vinegar, and water. Cover the pan and lightly simmer the ingredients for 5 minutes.

2 Rinse the cornichons and dice them finely. Peel and finely dice the onion. Add both to the pan and simmer for 10 minutes.

3 Remove the cores from the tomatoes. Pour boiling water over the tomatoes, and remove the skins with a paring knife. Cut the tomatoes in half, remove the seeds, and dice.

4 Add the tomatoes, sugar, salt, pepper, and tomato paste to the pan. Simmer the mixture, for 15-20 minutes, allowing the mixture to cook down and thicken. Remove the pan from the stove, stir in the sherry and cool. Before serving, season the chutney to taste with salt, sugar, pepper, and vinegar.

Onion Chutney

● low-cal
● sophisticated

Serves 4:
18 oz onions
1-2 fresh red chiles
2 tbs raisins
1/2 cup white wine vinegar
1/2 cup water
2 tbs honey
Salt to taste
1/2 tsp turmeric
2 whole cloves
Pinch of ground allspice
Pepper to taste

Prep time: 45 minutes
Per serving approx.: 85 calories / 2 g protein / 0 g fat / 21 g carbohydrates

1 Peel the onions. Depending on size, cut the onions into quarters or eighths, removing the root ends. Trim and rinse the chiles, and cut into paper-thin rings.

2 Put the onions and chiles in a saucepan with the raisins, vinegar, and water, place over medium heat, and bring to a boil. Stir in the honey, 1/2 tsp salt, the turmeric, cloves, and allspice.

3 Cook the mixture, uncovered, for 20-30 minutes, stirring occasionally, until it cooks down to a thick mixture. Let the chutney cool and season with salt and pepper.

Apple-Ginger Chutney

● inexpensive
● easy

Serves 4:
2 onions
18 oz tart apples
4 dried apricots
2 oz fresh ginger
2 tbs canola oil
5 tbs cider vinegar
3 tbs brown sugar
1/2 tsp ground coriander
Salt & pepper to taste
3 tbs water

Prep time: 50 minutes
Per serving approx.: 240 calories / 2 g protein / 4 g fat / 53 g carbohydrates

1 Peel and quarter the onions, and cut them into thin strips. Peel and quarter the apples, remove the cores, and slice. Finely chop the apricots. Peel the ginger and mince it finely.

2 In a saucepan, heat the oil over medium heat. Add the onions and sauté until translucent. Add the apples and sauté until softened. Stir in the apricots, vinegar, and sugar, and bring the mixture to a boil.

3 Add the ginger, coriander, salt, pepper, and water to the pan. Cook the mixture, uncovered, over medium heat for 20-30 minutes, stirring often, until it cooks down to a thick mixture. Let the chutney cool and season with salt and pepper.

Pineapple Chutney

● sophisticated
● can prepare in advance

Serves 4:
1 medium pineapple (about 2 lb)
1-2 fresh red chiles
1 oz fresh ginger
1 onion
5 tbs sugar
1/2 cup fresh lemon juice
Salt to taste
Freshly ground nutmeg to taste
2 tbs chopped almonds

Prep time: 50 minutes
Per serving approx.: 190 calories / 2 g protein / 3 g fat / 42 g carbohydrates

1 Peel the pineapple, remove the core and "eyes," and dice the fruit. Wash the chiles, remove the seeds, and slice them into thin rings. Peel and mince the ginger and the onion.

2 Melt the sugar in a saucepan until it becomes a light-caramel color. Add the lemon juice and stir with a wooden spoon until smooth. Add the pineapple, chiles, ginger, and onion. Cover the pan and simmer the mixture over medium heat for 25-30 minutes, stirring occasionally, until the mixture cooks down to a thick sauce.

3 Cool the chutney, and season with salt and nutmeg. Just before serving, fold in the chopped almonds.

Potato-Garlic Sauce

● inexpensive
● easy

Serves 4:
10 oz baking potatoes
3 cloves garlic
2 tbs ground almonds
1 tbs chopped fresh Italian parsley
1/4 cup extra-virgin olive oil
5–6 tbs vegetable or chicken stock
3–4 tbs fresh lemon juice
Salt to taste
6 black olives, pitted
Several leaves fresh Italian parsley for garnish

Prep time: 45 minutes
Per serving approx.: 145 calories / 3 g protein / 9 g fat / 14 g carbohydrates

1 Scrub the potatoes, cut them into large pieces, and cook them in their peels in just enough water to cover for 30 minutes. Drain the potatoes, plunge them into cold water, and remove the peels with a paring knife. Push the potatoes through a ricer or sieve into a bowl.

2 Peel and mince the garlic, and add it to the potatoes. Add the almonds, parsley, oil, 5 tbs stock, 3 tbs lemon juice, and a dash of salt. Stir vigorously until the potato mixture is light-colored and creamy. If necessary, add more stock and lemon juice to taste. Season with salt. Cover and refrigerate for at least 2 hours.

3 Before serving, cut the olives into slivers. Pour the potato-garlic sauce into a small bowl, sprinkle with the olives, and garnish with the parsley leaves. Serve slightly chilled, but not cold.

Variation
For a change of pace, mix in 2 tbs minced red bell pepper, or 2 tbs finely grated zucchini. Season the sauce to taste with salt and pepper, and stir in a little more stock or olive oil to keep it creamy.

Parsley-Walnut Pesto

● can prepare in advance
● sophisticated

Serves 4:
2 oz walnut halves
3 large bunches fresh Italian parsley
2 cloves garlic
2-oz hunk of Parmesan or Romano cheese
Salt to taste
About 1/2 cup extra-virgin olive oil
Pepper to taste

Prep time: 30 minutes
Per serving approx.: 375 calories / 14 g protein / 29 g fat / 20 g carbohydrates

1 Coarsely chop the walnuts. In a small nonstick skillet, brown the walnuts lightly, stirring until they become aromatic. Remove the walnuts from pan and let them cool.

2 Wash and shake dry the parsley. Remove the leaves from the stems and chop the leaves coarsely. Peel the garlic and chop it coarsely. Break or cut the cheese into small chunks.

3 To a blender, add the walnuts, parsley, garlic, cheese, 1/4 tsp salt, and about 1/4 cup of the olive oil and blend until a smooth mixture forms.

4 Gradually stir in the remaining 1/4 cup oil until a smooth, creamy paste is formed. Season the pesto with salt and pepper.

Variations
During the summer months, you can use fresh basil or even half parsley and half basil. You can also replace the walnuts with pine nuts, shelled hazelnuts, or even almonds.

Tip! Pesto is good prepared in advance. It's best to put it in screw-top jars, smooth the surface, and cover it with oil. Stored in this way, it will keep in the refrigerator for 2-3 weeks.

above: Parsley-Walnut Pesto
below: Potato-Garlic Sauce

Chocolate Fondue

● easy
● kids love it

Serves 4:
2 lb seasonal fruit (such as
  strawberries, cherries,
  peaches, nectarines,
  apples, pears, grapes,
  tangerines, bananas)
1/4 cup fresh lemon juice
2 oz slivered almonds
2 oz walnuts, finely
  chopped
4 oz Amaretti (Italian
  almond cookies)
8 oz semisweet chocolate
1 orange
1 cup heavy cream
Pinch of salt

Prep time: 30 minutes
Per serving approx.: 650 calories
/ 9 g protein / 40 g fat / 77 g
carbohydrates

1 Depending on the type,
wash or peel the fruit,
remove the seeds or core,
and cut into bite-sized
chunks. Sprinkle lemon
juice over peaches,
nectarines, apples, pears,
and bananas to prevent
discoloration. Arrange the
fruit on a serving dish.

2 Place the almonds,
walnuts, and Amaretti in
small bowls. Break the
chocolate into small
pieces. Wash and dry the
orange. Grate half of the
orange zest and squeeze
the juice.

3 In a saucepan, heat the
cream with the orange
juice, orange zest, and
salt. Add the chocolate
and melt while stirring
constantly over low heat.

4 Pour the chocolate
sauce into a small,
preheated dessert fondue
pot (or pretty saucepan),
and place it on the table
over the heat source.

5 To eat, spear the fruit
and amaretti with fondue
forks and dip in the
chocolate sauce. Let
excess sauce drip off and
dip in the slivered
almonds or walnuts.

Variation
If only adults are eating, you
can stir 2-3 tbs of brandy,
whisky, rum, or sherry, or
orange, peppermint or coffee
liqueur, into the cream before
adding the chocolate. You
can vary the type of
chocolate as desired, as well
as combine different types.

Exotic Coconut Fondue

● sophisticated
● low-cal

Serves 4:

7 oranges
4 limes (or 3 lemons)
4 oz grated coconut
1 baby pineapple (or 1/4
    large pineapple)
2 kiwis
1 carambola (star fruit)
1 papaya
1 mango
6 oz cape gooseberries
    (optional—increase other
    fruit if not using)
1 can coconut milk (14 oz)
2 tsp brown sugar

Prep time: 40 minutes
Per serving approx.: 275 calories
/ 5 g protein / 5 g fat / 70 g
carbohydrates

1 Wash and dry 2 of the oranges and 2 of the limes, and grate the zest. Squeeze the juice from all of the oranges and limes.

2 Divide the coconut among 4 small bowls.

3 Quarter the pineapple, remove the core, cut off the peel and the "eyes," and cut the fruit into bite-sized chunks. Peel the kiwis and cut them into eighths. Wash the carambola, slice it and, depending on its size, halve or quarter the slices.

4 Peel the papaya, halve it lengthwise, remove the seeds, and cut the fruit into cubes. Peel the mango, cut the fruit away from the pit, then cut the fruit into chunks. Remove the husks from the cape gooseberries (if using), wash them well, and cut them in half.

5 Arrange all of the fruit on a serving dish. Mix the orange juice and zest, lime juice and zest, coconut milk and sugar in a meat fondue pot, and heat while stirring constantly until steaming.

6 Place the fruit sauce on the table over the heat source. To eat, spear the fruit with fondue forks and dip into the hot sauce for about 2 minutes. Roll the fruit in the grated coconut.

Credits

Published originally under the title Fondues, ©1997
Gräfe und Unzer Verlag GmbH, Munich
English translation for the U.S. market ©2000,
Silverback Books, Inc.

Editor: Christine Wehling, Jennifer Newens
Reader: Christiane Kührt, Vené Franco
Translator: Christie Tam
Design and production: Shanti Nelson
Design: Heinz Kraxenberger
Production: Renate Hausdorf
Output: Helmut Giersberg
Photos: Reiner Schmitz; Teubner, p 8 (tomatoes);
p 17 (oil)
Food Stylist: Rudolf Vornehm

ISBN: 1-930603-40-1
Printed in Hong Kong through Global Interprint,
Santa Rosa, California.

Marlisa Szwillus
Szwillus inherited her love of cooking from her
parents, who stressed the value of good food and the
highest quality ingredients. Her joy in cooking and
eating continued to grow until her hobby became
her vocation. She first studied food science, then
became an editor in the cooking department of a
large women's magazine. For several years afterward,
she managed the cooking department of the largest
German food and household magazine. Since 1993,
she has been a freelance food journalist and
cookbook author.

Reiner Schmitz
Schmitz began his career in Düsseldorf and Munich,
Germany, as an assistant to various food and still life
photographers. In 1989, he became an independent
photo designer in these specialized areas. His
customers have included industry, advertising
agencies, and publishing houses. In particular,
Schmitz strives to produce photographs that enhance
the natural beauty of the food.